AT-A-GLANCE
2005
AT-A-GLANCE
2006
DAYMINDER
2007
AT-A-GLANCE
2008
I0813812
month AT·A GLANCE
1982
ACCOUNTS
CLOSED
2014
DAYMINDER
2015
DAYMINDER
2013
DAYMINDER
2012
AT-A-GLANCE
2011

The Inner Ear of Don Zientara

a half century of recording in one of America's most innovative studios, through the voices of musicians

composed by Antonia Tricarico

Published by Akashic Books

ISBN: 978-1-63614-092-6
Library of Congress Control Number: 2022947075

Photo editor: Antonia Tricarico
Designer: Kirk Waldroff

Front cover photo: Charles Steck, 1990/91.
Front endpapers: Inner Ear scheduling books, 1980–2020. Photos by Antonia Tricarico.
Back endpapers: Inner Ear scheduling calendars, January–October 2021. Photos by Antonia Tricarico.
Back cover photos: Antonia Tricarico, 2021.
Cover design assistance by Ian MacKaye.

Printed in China

Antonia Tricarico has been taking photos since 1997. She worked as a photo archivist for Lucian Perkins (a *Washington Post* Pulitzer Prize–winning photographer) and has collaborated with Tolotta Records, Dischord Records, Kill Rock Stars, and Youth Action Research Group. Her work can be found in private collections; in the Smithsonian Institution's National Museum of American History; the People's Archive in the Martin Luther King Jr. Memorial Library in Washington, DC; the Special Collections in Performing Arts in the Michelle Smith Performing Arts Library, University of Maryland; and the Collections of DC History Center, Washington, DC. Her photos have appeared in *Photo Review, Guitar World, Kerrang!, All Music, Chicago Reader,* the *Oregonian, Razorcake*, the *Quietus,* and *Fretboard Journal*. She is the creator of *Frame of Mind: Punk Photos and Essays from Washington, DC, and Beyond, 1997–2017*, also available from Akashic Books.

Table of Contents

Introduction

by Antonia Tricarico

Don Zientara was one of the first people I met on my initial visit to Washington, DC, in 1996. His studio, with CD and LP covers on the walls, photographs, paintings, framed articles, toys, games, books, stuffed animals, music magazines, DVDs, and, of course, all the equipment necessary to record a band, were all right there to make you feel like you were in your bedroom playing guitar or bass, or keeping the beat on a drum set sitting between a bookshelf and a big chair.

Over the following years, I did not spend much time in the Inner Ear Studio during recording sessions—it felt like I was intruding on someone else's creation. I kept myself out as much as possible, even with bands I knew well.

In my limited visits to Don's studio, he always welcomed me with snacks, coffee, and tea. It didn't matter whether you were there to record or not, he was invariably warm and friendly. While I was there, I was always impressed by the level of calm and respect shown. In my view, the bands and he had a simple understanding and willingness to exchange ideas. No deeper issues at play.

Don's critical feedback usually began with, "Are you sure you want to do that?" Motivating people to think about it, supporting their vision, but strongly questioning whether it was the right thing to do. Whether it was the first recording for a band or the fifth made no difference to Don. He wasn't thinking about the band winning some sort of award, he was there to make the music better regardless of who you were or who you intended to be. He definitely had pride in his work, and was never small-minded about it.

I've had many fantasies about being in a band and getting to work with Don. As a musician, I have only had one experience in a recording studio. In that session, it seemed like everyone felt they had the authority to tell me how to play the drums. (I've heard this from many female musicians.) But that wasn't the case with Don, as all the women in this book write. Don is an expert at nurturing your creativity without stepping on it.

In Don's studio, everyone felt free to express themselves, which may be one reason why they kept returning.

I was very honored when Don reached out to me and asked if I would make this book—and I immediately gave him an enthusiastic yes! So I asked numerous musicians to write short essays, and I was really happy with the responses I got. I love the variety in what people wrote—about Don, his contributions to their recordings, and especially the creative process. The photographs also convey what's so unique about Don and his studio. I would like to thank all the contributors whose words and images appear in this book.

Inner Ear may have closed its doors for business in October 2021 . . . but Don did not give up. He was wise enough to return to his original location—the basement of his home in Arlington, Virginia—to cheer up musicians young and old who thought the end of an era had arrived.

At Inner Ear Studio, the music never stops. All the different elements that Don fostered yielded a truly magical mixture, like fresh bread and olive oil: you can't go wrong.

Don Zientara interviewed by John Davis

June 21, 2021

Don Zientara (left) and John Davis at Inner Ear, June 2021. Photo by Antonia Tricarico.

John Davis: What would be the first thing that set you on this path to where you are today? I assume, in childhood, there was some sort of interest in sound or electronics. Can you recall what got you into it?

Don Zientara: Playing guitar. I started at about ten and I was living in Rochester, New York, in a Polish community, basically. My parents wanted me to take some music lessons, like parents do. "It'll be good for him." So, we went down to the music store. In Polish music, the crème de la crème of instruments is the accordion. And so, of course, they had accordion lessons, but at the time I really lucked out because Elvis Presley was coming on the scene and he was a guitar player. So they were offering guitar lessons and I thought, *Accordion? Guitar? Accordion? Guitar? Nah, I'll take guitar* [*laughs*]. So I started on that. And just being naturally curious about how to amplify things and use PAs and things like that, I wanted to find out more about them, and to do so you need to get into bands. Okay, you got to play somewhere. Okay, where's your microphone? Where's your PA and all that stuff? Where's your amplifier? We scrounged around on trash days looking at all this stuff that people threw out. We'd see if we could salvage what was there. That was the era of Magnavox stereos, so there was a lot of good stuff. I dabbled in that and I had friends who really knew something about electronics at the time and they helped me out. I remember we pulled an amplifier from this receiver and made it into a guitar amplifier. And we used the box we built and sawed it up and put a couple speakers in there that were in the Magnavox thing, and there's our speaker. And I continued through that whole thing. Went to college, Syracuse University, and then went for my graduate degree at Morgantown, West Virginia University, in art. Don't ask me why I picked art, but once you start . . .

Don Zientara, 1974. Photo courtesy of Don Zientara.

Ravenstone, 1975. (Left to right) Gary Smith, Don Zientara, Mandinga, Robert Goldstein, and Laurie Hyde. Photo courtesy of Don Zientara.

No Joe at Madams Organ, 1979. Mark Hoback (left), Don Zientara (center), Andy Charneco (right). Photo courtesy of Don Zientara.

Davis: What branch of art?

Zientara: Painting and printmaking. Okay, very lucrative fields! [*Laughter*] Ask Vincent van Gogh. But at the time, once I got out of Syracuse, that was the draft lottery time, and this is 1970 and the Vietnam War's going on, and my lottery number was number one. Pretty much you're guaranteed to be picked. So, when I went to West Virginia University, I told the local draft board, "Hey, I couldn't have the physical examination in Rochester because I was living in Morgantown, West Virginia." So the draft board arranged stuff in their bureaucratic way. During Christmas vacation, I said, "I'm back in Rochester. I can't do it in Morgantown. Can you schedule it for Rochester?" By the summer, to make a long story short, I finally passed my physical and the draft board finally got me. I looked into the army's career choices and discovered they had a program for guaranteed training in a number of fields. One field was electronics. I'd never had electronics training. But since I had already fooled around with amps and tape recorders and speakers and stuff, I figured I'd get some formal training. That's what I signed up for. After army basic training, I was sent to electronics school. I just sat there for a couple months. Finally, I got called into the office and was told, "Look, there's a lot of people who have signed up for electronics training. We'll get you in," because the army will honor its promise, "but chances are, after you graduate from electronics school, you'll probably be made a cook or something like that." But then I was told, "They've got this position for someone who paints posters in Alexandria, Virginia: do you want to do that?" I was thinking, *The rice paddies of Vietnam or Alexandria, Virginia?* [*Laughter*] And so I was posted to Alexandria and did graphic arts for a couple of years.

Davis: What year did you move here?

Zientara: '72 or '73, somewhere in that area. I don't remember exact dates. But all the while, you know, when I got here, the first thing I do is look for people to join a band with.

Davis: Had you been playing in bands the whole time?

Zientara: After the army posted me to Alexandria, Virginia, I was able to pursue music when I was off duty. And that's how I met Robert Goldstein. We got together and started Ravenstone. It was a good gig. Really a lot of fun. But all good things come to an end. I got out of the army and worked for a very short time at Woodward & Lothrop [department store], the frame shop there. From there, I went to the National Gallery of Art.

Davis: Also framing?

Zientara: Framing, conservation for prints and drawings. Because I knew inks and paper real well. I did that for about five years. And at the five-year point, they were giving us staff a tour of a lot of the new places in the gallery. One of the things they were doing was building a recording studio for the acoustic guided tours. And they were having trouble wiring this thing up. I said, "Here's what you got to do. You just do this, put this together, and it's done." They said, "Well, why don't you become the audio engineer here?" So I just flipped careers. And for the next five years, I was the Gallery's audio engineer. Lectures, notes for the concerts, anything for which they needed recording. Audio for videotaped programs, or anything like that. Then I left the Gallery and went to work managing a studio. I just didn't like that at all because basically it wasn't hands-on.

Davis: The administrative side of running a studio.

Zientara: Yeah, pushing papers, basically. I think I was there for about four months. A very short amount of time. But in the meantime I spent every spare moment recording in my basement. Finally, I resigned from the commercial studio and focused on Inner Ear full-time. Still in the basement. And then, in 1990, I leased a more spacious location.

Davis: When did you start calling it Inner Ear?

Zientara: Well, it was kind of like Zientara's base . . . Studio B from my home's basement for a long while. I didn't really name it anything. One of my engineers just started calling it Inner Ear.

DANCE
Featuring
RAVENSTONE
$1.00 admission
FREE BEER
9pm-1am
Friday June 20
New South
Faculty Lounge

Flyer for a Ravestone show at Gallaudet University, Washington, DC, 1974/75.

Davis: Do you remember who that was?

Zientara: No, unfortunately I don't remember who it was. He went on to work at Wolf Trap, where he was the engineer for a long while. But I don't remember who it was exactly.

Davis: Your connection to the DC punk scene, does that come from Skip Groff?

Zientara: It does! I mean, it was pure luck. Pure dumb luck. Robert [Goldstein] was also a big part of me getting into the punk scene because when Ravenstone broke up, he went into more forward-looking bands like the Look

Studio B drums, 1975. Photo courtesy of Don Zientara.

Studio B, 1975. Photo courtesy of Don Zientara.

and, of course, Urban Verbs. The Look was playing at some place and the Slickee Boys were playing with them. And Robert said, "Hey, can you record our band?" So I went there with a tape recorder. I had stereo tape, recording vocals on one channel and the band on the other. And Martin "Kim" Kane of the Slickee Boys came up and said, "Hey, you got some extra tape here, record us!" I had extra tape, so I recorded them. Little did I know that Skip Groff was kind of their manager at the time. So when they came over to mix, Skip accompanied them. He liked the way I operated, so he called me up and said, "I met these guys, Bad Brains, and they want to record." So they came over. Then, a little further down the line, Skip said, "I know these other kids I could send over there called the Teen Idles." So they came over. And, I mean, everything just started happening.

Davis: That Bad Brains recording, I've heard the story about Skip passing off production duties to Kim Kane and then Bad Brains only having something like an hour to record. What are your memories of that day?

Zientara: It just . . . flashed by. They just came in, they set up quickly, we recorded everything, and that was the album. That was it. I can't remember if we mixed it the same day, but we may have. And it was just very, very, very quick. They were, you know, full speed ahead.

Davis: Was there any sort of bond with Bad Brains? Did it feel like, creatively, you were working together, or were you more like a vessel at that point? What was your role?

Zientara: Yeah, definitely, I was an outsider. First of all, I was not of their generation or any of the punks at that time. And secondly, my style of music was not that [*laughter*]. It was sort of like, *What the heck is this?*

Davis: Did you like it?

Zientara: After a while, I did. Yeah, I mean, at first it was, it was kind of, you know, *Is this art?* But then I realized that it had qualities. Number one of them was just the energy behind it. That was great. And it was kicking back at a lot of things that were going on from California and the West Coast at that time. So it had value. Had a lot of value. So eventually I grew to like it and I wanted to capture what was there and I looked to what they wanted to get out of it. I sort of geared my recording process to the way they wanted to get it out. There was not the focus on technicalities or anything else. We just went in and we had fun. We just did this stuff quickly and then we could judge it afterward. Or maybe not judge it afterward. But basically, we just did it. And, of course Ian MacKaye was a big part of it too. Talk about Mr. Quickness. I mean, he just rushes through stuff.

Davis: The first time you worked with Ian, did it seem like there was a rapport there right away? Not that you would say, "I'm going to be working with this guy in forty years . . ."

Zientara: I didn't know him at all. Ian related this story to me years, years, years later: they're coming over in the car, crossing over from DC, and I guess none of them have ever been to Virginia.

Davis: Crossing the river!

Zientara: Yeah, [*laughs*] across the river. And now they're saying to themselves, "I wonder if they have 7-Elevens" [*laughter*]. But it was just a totally new experience for them. I was kind of removed from it in the sense that, especially with Teen Idles in the early days, I was just sort of standing back and wondering, *Okay, what is this?*

Davis: When did you feel like you started to become more of a part of the creative process with the bands?

Zientara: Well, I was always part of the creative process, in terms of the mechanics of it.

Davis: From working with you many times in the studio, I think of you as another voice in the crew. We are a group together making this record—the band, you, Ian. And I guess that's what I'm sort of getting at, you know? When did you become more a part of that other side of the creative process?

Zientara: Probably very soon after we moved here. Because at that point, I really wanted to just immerse myself totally. I would speak up and talk about the songs, talk about what they're doing. Or ask them questions about it if I didn't understand. And then just try to help it out as much as possible. I mean, my whole goal is to make it tangible to the audience. I looked at it like, "Okay, *you* like this. But how are other people going to look at it? Let's get it so that it's attractive to them." Even now, I have a radio show—along with my cohost, Alex Vidales—called *StageCraft*. It focuses on performers. They have their art, but how do you get the art out to the audience? And it's a very, very tough thing. That in itself is an art. So, you know, you could write the songs but if they aren't presented in a way that people could latch on and just enjoy them fully, then you're kind of missing out on it a little bit. And that goes for all kinds of, not just musicians, it goes for comedians, actors, anyone who goes up onstage, basically.

Davis: Who have been some of your closest collaborators over this journey? Obviously, you've worked with so many people—Ian is someone who jumps to mind. But who else?

Zientara: I'm not sure if "collaboration" is the right word. Because that is almost like we are creating this art together. And I was almost like looking at what they have and fine-tuning different areas. So if someone came in here with a song they wanted to record, I may have suggestions about different aspects of it or different phrasing and lyrics or how to sing and what kind of guitars to put on and things like that. But it was *their* baby. So, collaboration is kind of a strong word. I never really felt like a collaborator. A helper more than anything else.

Davis: [*Laughs*] Okay.

Zientara: A facilitator!

Davis: Right, and I think I'm projecting my own experience onto that question. I remember those questions you would ask. And you would frame it in a way that was very

Mixer built by Don in 1982. Photo by Antonia Tricarico.

respectful and just kind of inquisitive. "So, why are you doing it this way?" or "Why did you want to try this?" I just remember that being very helpful. Like, "How can I explain why we're trying to do?" And sometimes you can't, so maybe we should rethink this? If I'm projecting it's because I think we worked together to make these records under the band's name.

Zientara: I don't want that art to die on the vine. It's got to appeal to people. And with punk art, sometimes that's a challenge. Because, especially in the early days, you're overcoming a lot of biases and judgments. But, you know, if it's gonna survive at all, it's gonna have to appeal. I was just looking at, you know, "Is this going to work? How's it going to sound to the guy in the street?"

Davis: And how often do you feel you were able to be effective at that?

Zientara: Well, there's a lot of bands that did die on the vine [*laughter*]. A lot of records that did . . .

Davis: That's unavoidable.

Zientara: Oh, absolutely unavoidable. Yeah, I didn't lose sleep over it. But I figured I gave it my best shot and what I had to offer. I guess it's a production role in a sense, although I always let the bands know that, you know, either you've got a producer or you are producing as a group or we're producing it as a group, because we're all making decisions on these whole things. I would ask, "How are you going to sell it? Are you going to tour with it or, you know, what cities are you going to hit?" . . . all those little questions. It all makes sense, because that gets them thinking about, "Okay, once we're finished with this, then what are we gonna do?" Which is a big one.

Davis: You mentioned Bad Brains and Teen Idles. As far as the basement studio space, what are some other memories that come to mind for you?

Zientara: Well, those were very cyclone-type years. And at first we had the control room on the side, our side porch, and I had a big snake going down to the basement. We're in a furnace room that was probably about this wide to the wall. It was a totally windowless room that had a furnace, water heater, and a lot of plumbing stuff, and of course, all the gear . . . and no air-conditioning. On warm days, we would mix Minor Threat and we'd be down to our underwear, just sweating bullets. And once you were almost getting too dizzy where you can't make judgments, the mix was finished. And we were working with some equipment that was kind of sketchy. Radio Shack microphones or anything else I could dig up that really worked. I had a mixer that I built myself, which was actually pretty good. It's still up in the attic of the house. And I experimented a lot. I like to experiment with bands, because that was some of the reason why I want to record them. I want to try this out with them and try that out and try this technique and that technique to see if it worked for them. Once again, always looking at: after the recording, what next? So that's what we did down there. I know Ian would bring in bands. Jeez, you know, bringing one band one day, one band another day, another band another day. We very rarely did three or four days in a row. Very rarely. Just very, very quick. And I would say successful in the sense that they felt it was homey enough where they could let go. But any kind of specific memory? First of all, there wasn't a window when we first moved into the basement. It was literally the furnace room. And there was a door to it. And that's . . . it was a cell, basically [*laughter*]. And there was no window into the next room over where the band would play. All we had was a talkback mic.

Davis: When did you change that?

Zientara: Eventually, I cut through the wall and just put a window in. But it was years and years later. I just didn't think of who's going to take off or not or what was going to happen. I mean, the punk music, how long is it gonna stay around? Can't be around too long? Six months, maybe, then it'll be gone? [*Laughter*]

Davis: Roughly what percentage of what you were recording was punk or new wave or related to that scene?

Zientara: A huge percentage. The Slickee Boys had, you know, they brought some surf rock bands in but they're almost kind of punky surf rock, right? Beatnik Flies, Insect Surfers.

Davis: So, moving into this studio space in 1990, I assume you just felt you'd outgrown the basement space? Did someone approach you with this space?

Zientara: Oh, no. I'd been looking for a number of years. Because it was obvious that, you know, the house I'm in, you could hear it all over the house. I mean, they played loud. One of the things we enjoyed was that they would play the way they would perform. And I felt that brought out the best of them. And if it brought out the best of them, that's the way we're gonna do it. And once again, we're looking toward the end product here, making sure that it sounds good. So I had to move out. And I looked, looked, and looked, and I found this space. I guess there was a sign up in the window or something. I checked next door, which was WETA public television, until it was Arlington County. And they had recording studios in there for voice-over and things like that. So I went there and talked with their engineers. "How is this area for recording?" They said it's the best because you've got the big hill between here and the large radio transmitting towers in Tenleytown [DC]. No interference, no radio or taxi cabs or any kind of stuff like that. And he said it's just terrific. So, I bit. I came in here and set up and a lot of the fish on the walls in the studio area, they were from the very beginning because I had big walls with nothing on them. We were at a school play, kindergarten play, and I said, "Can I have these fish when you're finished with 'em?" He said, "Sure, yeah, get rid of them."

Davis: So, you don't even know exactly who painted those?

Zientara: No, it was just the kindergarten class. Probably the teacher in the classes.

Davis: The other paintings in here, how many of them are yours?

Zientara: A number of them there, but a lot of other people too. I have a lot from Jay Stuckey, who's a painter out in California.

Davis: Who was also a musician? He was in Your Majesty and Thee Evolution Revolution, I think?

Zientara: I can't remember the band. And it was, you know, they came and they went.

Davis: I feel you told me once that someone from Nation of Ulysses built the drum riser.

Zientara: Yes. That was before one of the Fugazi albums, I do not remember which album it was. But Steve Gamboa from Nation of Ulysses, I contracted him to build the riser. NOU were on tour and Steve figured they would come back and he'd build the riser just before Fugazi was going to record. Back to back, the tour and Fugazi. Well, I guess NOU came back at, like, three in the morning. So, Steve was in here groggy-eyed, building it, and Fugazi was moving their equipment in. So he built the riser, yes. And it really worked well by us. I didn't have a riser for a good four or five years, at least. It was just the concrete floor, which is terrific. I mean, one of the things that's nice about this is there's nothing below us. Upstairs is storage, right? There is the alley directly outside. So the isolation was perfect. I really couldn't make any noise that would bother people.

Davis: Who are some of the other people who have their fingerprints on this space? You just mentioned Steve building the riser. Are there other aspects of this space that other people were involved in?

Zientara: Well, there were the carpenters that built it. I hired this guy, and he had a crew of a few people. But other than that, everything was just sort of tacked on afterward. A lot of stuff is found objects. The chair you're sitting in, actually, all three of those chairs are found. My whole office is almost stocked with stuff I found in the trash. You know, it's some good stuff.

Davis: That's a theme going back to the beginning.

Zientara: Absolutely, absolutely.

Davis: So, it's been just over thirty years in this space. How long has this mixing board been here?

Zientara: The original board was a Tascam 52. And the original recorder was the Fostex B-16. And then, around 1994, I got this board and the twenty-four tracks. I had outgrown the other things.

Davis: This second phase of Inner Ear is a very long one. From this space, what are some of the things that stand out to you?

Zientara: Gee, there's just so many little incremental things. I remember one of the things was when Fugazi was doing one of their albums, I think it was *Red Medicine*, not sure. We'd be recording for about twelve hours a day. So after they left, I would be pulling out the modules in there with my soldering gun and recapping the entire board. And that went on for the entire album. It took a long while to recap it. That was, you know, that was incredibly . . . just memorable. And a lot of the bands that came through here, they really just brought a certain energy to it that stimulated me to want to record them and to be here and to get something good that they can go home with.

Davis: So, would you say the studio is closing or you're moving?

Zientara: Good question. Probably moving, but in another phase, which will have less room. Probably just enough room to do drums, if at all. And during the pandemic, I was doing a lot of remote mixing and mastering. I've got a studio set up at my home. Everywhere I go, I set up a studio it seems [*laughter*], and I was doing a lot of work there. That seemed to work out incredibly well and we got really great results. That seems to be building up and I've done a lot of international mixing for people who send me files. Of course, you know, it's easy these days to get that out. So, it'll be more centered on that aspect of things, where you can do it in the control room. As far as a studio area, not so much.

Opposite: four-track recorder (1979) from Inner Ear donated by Don to the DC Punk archive at the Martin Luther King Jr. Memorial Library, Washington, DC. Photo by Antonia Tricarico.

Yesterday and Today Records
Skip Groff founded Yesterday and Today Records in 1977. He became a central figure in supporting local punk bands by releasing their music on his Limp Records label, promoting other labels, and providing employment to members of many local bands.
6
Lunch Meat
Mission Impossible
7
8
D.C.'s first punk record, Slickee Boys, Hot and Cool, Dacoit Records 197
Donated by Matt Moffatt
DC Punk Archive
TEAC A-2340SX
4 channel SIMUL-SYNC stereo
POWER
SPEED
OUTPUT
VU
REC
STOP
PAUSE
PLAY
RECORD
RECORD MODE
PHONES
Inner Ear Studio
Inner Ear Studio, located in Arlington, Virginia, was founded in the late 1970s by musician and recording engineer Don Zientara. His devotion to capturing a band's live energy in a recording and to the local music community made Inner Ear essential support for local bands navigating the recording process.
Four-track recorder from Inner Ear Studio
Donated by Don Zientara
DC Punk Archive

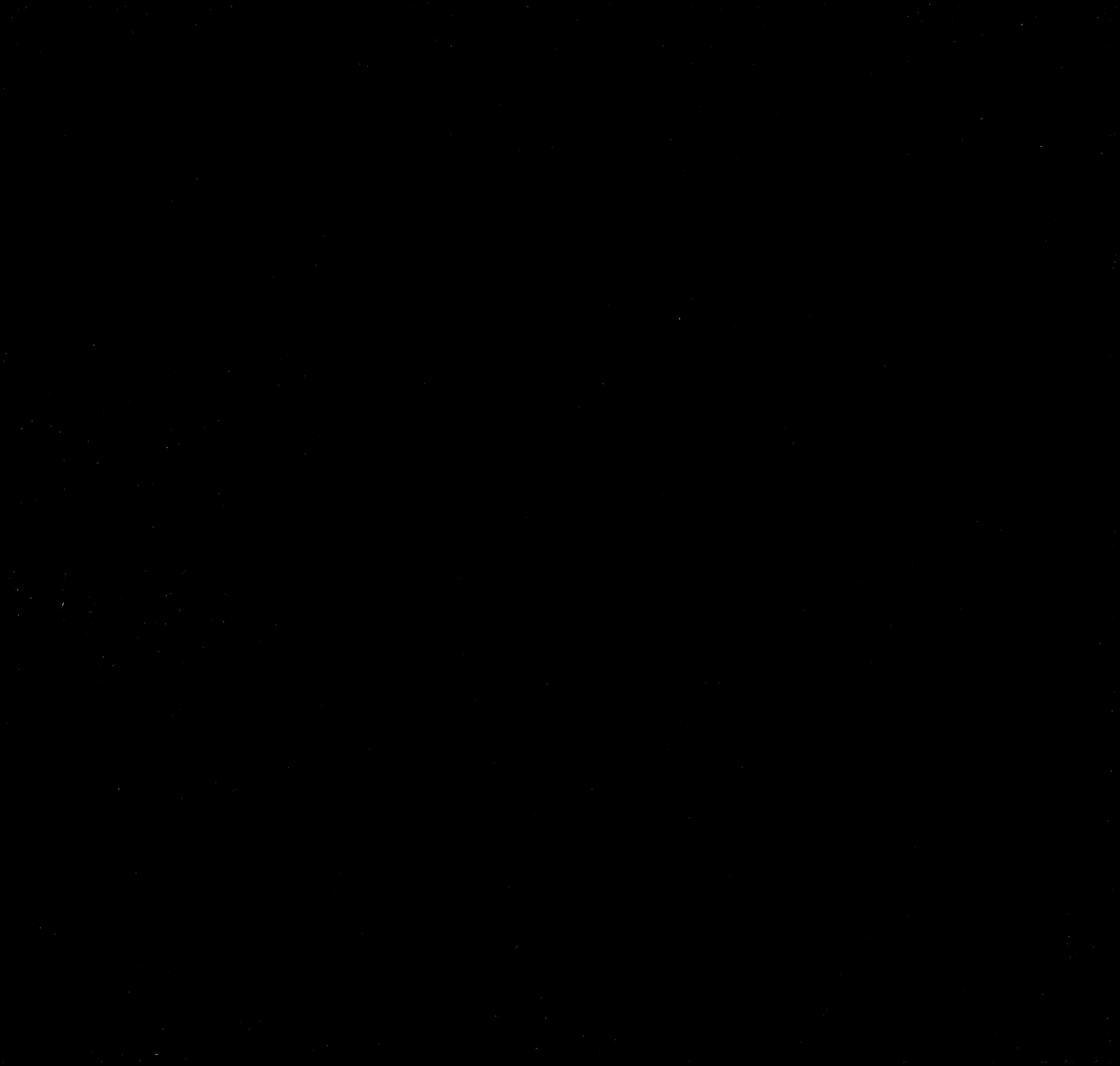

Part I

The Basement Years (1972-1989)

The Slickee Boys

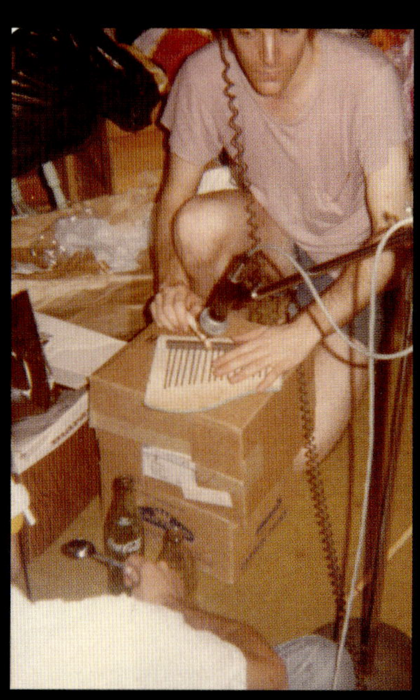

The Slickee Boys, *Third EP* session, 1979. TOP LEFT: Kim Kane. Photo courtesy of the Slickee Boys. TOP CENTER-LEFT: Mark Noone. Photo by Kim Kane. TOP CENTER-RIGHT: Marshall Keith. Photo by Kim Kane. TOP RIGHT: Marshall Keith playing the toy piano and Dan Palensky playing the Coke bottles. Photo by Kim Kane. BOTTOM LEFT: Dan Palensky. Photo by Kim Kane. BOTTOM RIGHT: Ted Niceley (top left), Skip Groff (bottom left), and Don Zientara. Photo by Kim Kane.

Kim Kane

The Slickee Boys

Don Zientara and Inner Ear Studio—normally strange or strangely normal?

Here was a straight-looking, really tall (and I'm six one and I had to look way up!), but nice guy. Here he is recording us fringe, weirdo musicians playing DIY punk, arty, and DIY new wave.

We'd pull up to this "studio," and unexpectedly this nice normal older house. Added to that first impression is the basement with Emily's toys and stuff.

It was funny since his recorders were upstairs in which I called Studio A and we would have to yell/talk back and forth from the basement, or Studio B.

I never saw anything faze Don or get him upset, unlike stories you hear about "famous" producers/engineers.

Any sound was a go. For example, for a song called "Reverse Psychiatry," Don let Marshall play a little toy piano, and Dan play water-filled Coke bottles on the floor, he miked it! But no session started without Don doing his famous slow, meticulous cleaning of the heads with those long Q-tips!

The Slickee Boys were the second band recorded by Don. It was at the American University Tavern live—after seeing him do the Look that same night.

I also recorded the Bad Brains first ever recording session at Inner Ear for Skip Groff of Yesterday and Today and his label Limp Records.

The band showed up so late that we had to record the seven songs all at once, quickly in a row. Then Don and I sat in the control room and Gary had to do all his lead overdubs also in a row. We tried to adjust his fuzz box/boost box but it was permanently stuck full-on!

Don was an honor to work with, and think of all the cool sounds that came out of Inner Ear.

Mark Noone

The Slickee Boys

I remember every recording session I had at Inner Ear was extremely pleasant. I had done some recording with a band of high school chums in a friend's basement. We never seemed to get it right.

I joined the Slickee Boys in the winter of '78 and we recorded what we refer to as the *Third EP* with Don, Ted Niceley, and Skip Groff. We were cramped in the little basement room which was the studio and then the adjacent room which was the control room. It was very fun but serious. There were toys everywhere, and we used the basement bathroom as the vocal booth. As I was waiting to record my vocals, I snooped around a bit in the bathroom waiting for my cue, and there in the shower was a jumbo Gibson guitar and a surfboard!

Don, a surfer, was usually barefoot in the studio and was willing to try anything. Nothing was off the table. "Want to try the vocals outside?" "How about adding a police siren in this section?" That *Third EP* was my first real recording. We recorded and mixed it there. We sometimes had up to eight people in the little control room where Don had two Macintosh tube amplifiers throwing off a lot of heat. It could get pretty close in there.

We went in later to the new larger studio near Alexandria for other projects.

I remember working with Joey P, Eddie Janney, and of course Don. I recently listened to a single (two songs) I produced there with a band called Vinyl Gentleman. It still stands up very well.

I still feel lucky to run into Don from time to time, it's always good to see him; we talk about surfing, his (grown) kids, and even recording.

Dan Palenski

The Slickee Boys

I had just joined the Slickee Boys in '77 and we were playing at the Keg. I saw this tall, thin guy to the right of the stage with a tape recorder on a table. He was busy hanging microphones over the stage, looping them over the lighting truss. These weren't like the big professional microphones, but the black plastic ones on a skinny cord. I asked Kim Kane, "Who is this guy?" He then introduced me to Don. I recognized the name because I had just done the (yet-unreleased) Separated Vegetables LP cover print/typesetting for Kim and remembered his name, because he had recorded the live parts of the LP. Don said he was just recording the night's show for reference, like kind of a practice run to learn from and make improvements on.

Kim said Don was now recording in his basement, so we did the EP for Skip Groff's new label there ('78). I remember driving through the neighborhood of post-WWII brick Cape Cods to his house. We set up in his basement amid his daughter Emily's toys. I used her toy chest to hold my kick drum in place on the tile floor. The four-track was upstairs in a small library room off of the living room. It sat on a walnut rack table. There was no talkback mic between upstairs and downstairs, so Martha had to run to the bottom of the basement steps and yell upstairs for Don to turn the machine on between each take. After a take, we would all run upstairs and sit around on the floor as Don played it back. Marshall was the most adept musician in the band and I remember him and Don brainstorming on how to bounce tracks to get all the overdubs in. Don's relaxed and friendly demeanor made the whole project fun and he was a wizard at track bouncing. It was like just rehearsing in your parents' basement and hanging out.

We returned to do the *Third EP* ('79) there with Skip Groff as producer. Skip, Ted, and Don all got along and everything went smoothly. In all my years I have never heard anyone say anything bad about Don. That is quite an amazing accomplishment in these parts. I did some drum tracks at Don's for Mark Hoback's *A Sides* LP ('80). I was chatting with Don and I told him Christmas was coming up and I didn't have any oplatek for Christmas Eve dinner. Like me, Don is Polish and he knew what I was talking about. He said, "Maybe I can help." The next night I came in to record and he handed me an envelope of oplatek. I have met many people in my life who say, "Maybe I can help," as just conversation filler, but if Don said it he followed through, and that is rare. It is probably why I still remember it today.

We recorded the *Cybernetic Dreams of Pi* LP ('83) at Don's and a few outtakes. By this time he had a roughed-out booth in the basement. I love this record because Don really captured what we were doing. After this we were sucked down the small-record-label rabbit hole, but the making of that record with Don stands as one of the most exciting experiences of my life.

Martha Hull

Reind Dears - The Slickee Boys

My fondest thoughts of Don have to do with his early "field recordings" of the Slickee Boys's original and second lineups, live at the Keg and at the Psyche Delly. Those are records of a golden time for us. That Don was even interested in capturing what we were doing—as green and sloppy and raw as we were—was pretty exciting, and he had that unique combination of intense enthusiasm and utter calm, way back then. Would we call his mobile recording unit "Outer Ear"? I dunno, but I'm still grateful.

Danny Frankel

Reind Dears

Should we separate the musician from the music?

I say no. The musician interprets the music through his, her experiences.

Do you feel that your creativity is snatched away from you when you walk into the studio from your practice space?

No way, you do your thing.

Don never said to us anything along the lines of, "Okay, what I am hearing is . . ." or, "Okay, the last guy did this . . ." Ha! Unless it seemed like we needed direction.

What should you do to ensure that the integrity of your original work will be preserved, and won't be jeopardized by the studio technical environment?

When we recorded at Don's it wasn't overthought, and I remember it was a fun afternoon, but it can get creative with the technical stuff, with mic placement, and sounds and effects.

Henry Rollins

SOA - Rollins Band

As best as I can remember, I met Don when the Teen Idles went to Inner Ear, Don's home studio, to record what would become the *Minor Disturbance* EP, produced by Skip Groff and the first record released by Dischord. I was amazed that this low-profile environment was the same place that had produced the Bad Brains recordings that would eventually comprise the *Black Dots* LP. When I say home studio, I mean it. Inner Ear was a house, with children's toys and all the things you might expect in a modest suburban Virginia dwelling. This is where Don's innovative brilliance came into play. Instruments were arranged strategically to allow the band to work comfortably within the conventional confines, complete with neighbors. Once the tape was rolling, it was all studio.

Don immediately inspired confidence and camaraderie with the Teen Idles. He was obviously bright and his enthusiasm for the project was as infectious as it was genuine. Watching him work with the band, it occurred to me that this is the way musicians, either new to the studio process or well acquainted, would deliver at optimum levels. They were respected and not put in a position of having to defend their work at the critical moment. Don made the whole experience fun and energized. The record really sounds like the Teen Idles. Obviously, to a great extent it's because it's them playing, but as important, the setting was such that they weren't having to think about anything else and not made to feel self-conscious. I'm willing to bet that many bands were able to really turn it loose because of how welcoming Don is to musicians and what they hope to achieve. Months later, I was back at Inner Ear making a record that would become the second Dischord release, SOA's *No Policy* EP.

You might hear this from more than one person: I have never met anyone like Don Zientara.

I've known Don over forty years and he remains perpetually curious, buoyant, and very much "If the glass is half full, we can work with that" optimistic. Besides being a top-shelf, innovative engineer, he lives to capture sound. Before a band comes into the studio, their music is only partially existent. If it's not recorded, then it's not completely provable. If someone can't hear it, then it's so many trees falling in the forest. You can go into any studio and find the means to record sound, but no matter how great the gear is, without a skilled engineer, you're compromised from the start. As technically adept as Don is, it's how he runs a session that makes it happen. So many truly memorable records have come out of Inner Ear.

One of the most fascinating collaborative relationships in independent music I know of is the multidecade span and prolific output of Don and Ian MacKaye. When you see all the records they have made together, you might conclude that neither had done anything else. I've had the privilege of watching them work together.

Countless bands have benefited from Don Zientara and Inner Ear Studio. We music fans have him to thank for countless hours of music that we have played over and over. To say that Don has permanently impacted music culture is not overstatement but fact. Pretty cool.

Lyle Preslar
Minor Threat

Minor Threat wrote some songs in the fall of 1980—actually, Ian and Jeff had written songs, and Brian and I messed with them for bit. We rehearsed (we called it "practice") those songs a lot. At some point we decided to record them.

I'd seen pictures of recording studios in rock and roll magazines like *Creem*; these were all Zeppelin, Eagles, the Who—full-tilt affairs with huge mixing consoles, stacked racks of devices that surely made everything sound good, tape machines always at the ready to catch any genius riffs, and above all: GLASS. Panoramic glass windows fronted the control rooms; glass separated the vocal booths from the studio; glass separated the producers and mixers from the musicians. It was double-paned, fully insulated, wraparound: special glass for special people.

One evening in 1981 we went to record. Strangely, this place in Virginia we drove up to looked to me just like a suburban tract house, nothing like the *Creem* scene. Carrying my meager guitar stuff down a flight of stairs into the basement, I discovered that the "studio" was mainly a kid's playroom, the "control room" was a furnace closet, and the "vocal booth" was a laundry room. I wasn't in any position to be disappointed, but hell, I thought our producer Don wouldn't be able to see us playing because there wasn't any glass. No GLASS. I felt sorry for me, I felt sorry for Don. He had a studio bereft of glass. All he could do was HEAR us. All we could do was hear him in our headphones. No glass for anyone.

I'm not sure how, but it all worked out that session—and it worked out for a few years after that. Don seemed to be okay with no glass. He heard us. He wasn't much to look at. Neither were we. Enough. And as anyone who listens can easily tell, he was Minor Threat's secret weapon, like all great producers are for their bands.

Inner Ear would get glass later, I'm told.

And so what?

Steve Hansgen
Minor Threat - Poisonous H

The first time I can remember seeing any mention of Don Zientara was on the back cover of the third Slickee Boys EP. The credit simply read, *Zientara "B" Studio*. Not *Inner Ear*.

I love that record. It opened a lot of doors for me that had previously seemed closed. And being both a budding musician and producer, I paid attention to and loved how the record sounded.

I had no notion, at fifteen, that I would be lucky enough to be associated with this enigmatically named personage, Don Zientara, for the next forty years. And hopefully well beyond.

But lucky I am.

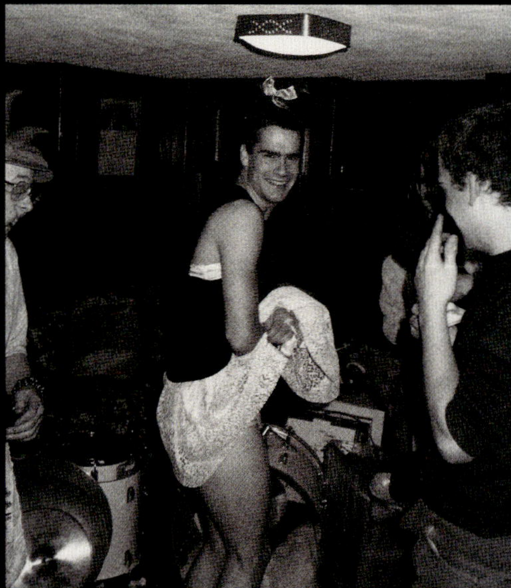

TOP LEFT: Minor Threat with Don Zientara, *Out of Step* session, 1983. Top row (left to right): Steve Hansgen and Don Zientara, bottom row (left to right): Jeff Nelson, Ian MacKaye, Brian Baker, and Lyle Preslar. Photo by Richard Moore. B&W PHOTOS: recording a demo at their first Inner Ear session in 1981. (They returned to the studio a month or two later to record their first 7".) TOP RIGHT: Lyle Preslar, Brian Baker, and Ian MacKaye. Photo by Skip Groff. BOTTOM LEFT: Ian MacKaye. Photo by Skip Groff. BOTTOM CENTER: Brian Baker, Henry Rollins, and Ian MacKaye. Photo by Skip Groff. BOTTOM RIGHT: Brian Baker and Jeff Nelson. Photo by Skip Groff.

By the time I reached eighteen, Inner Ear had become a holy place to me. In his South Arlington basement, Don had recorded some of my favorite and now historically relevant records ever.

And so it was to this basement I came in January of 1983, to record the most historically relevant record of my "career."

Upon arrival, Don was, as always, warm, helpful, patient, and hilarious. The vibe at Inner Ear has never been "all work." The atmosphere was relaxed and, back then, filled with his children's toys. I was in punk rock heaven.

The band set up and we got our sounds pretty quickly. We were ready to record in an hour or so. We cut all of the basic tracks "live" to Don's Tascam eight-track recorder. Vocals, guitars, bass, and drums. Every song was done in one take, except one that needed two takes. We were done and out in around in four hours. With the exception of a few overdubs done over the next few days and mixing, we were done recording.

Having never made a record before, I simply figured that this was how it was done. All these years later, I still do.

God bless you, Don Zientara. You're the best teacher and mentor ever. It has been one of the true honors of my life to work with you and call you my friend.

Rob Moss

Artificial Peace

Artificial Peace's lack of experience as musicians didn't hold us back from forming a band, or making music. If anything, it was like a dare. And we used that energy to push us. We practiced in Mike's basement. We played basement shows. We thrived in that environment.

Maybe that's why recording at Inner Ear, which at the time was in Don's basement, was perfect. We might've felt intimidated had we gone to a more professional studio. Or maybe it would've gone to our heads? Don and Ian understood that. They created a balance between the urgency of recording and mixing seventeen songs in an afternoon and the informality of making it seem like just another day in the basement. That balance was critical. Perhaps that's what made Inner Ear such a great place to record basement bands like ours.

I never got to do a session at Inner Ear after Don moved the studio out of his basement. But his website referred to ". . . providing a casual, comfortable space for people to create and record music." I'm sure that's correct. I would've liked to have experienced it for myself.

John Mortimer, the barrister and author, said, "Farce is tragedy played at a thousand revolutions per minute." How farcical that Inner Ear was shuttered to make way for an arts center. But I'm glad that so many of Don's recording sessions—whether they were made in his basement or his studio on Oakland Street—will survive. Which is why we make records in the first place. They're evidence of our past in a permanent form.

Brian Gay
Government Issue

In July 1981 the members of Government Issue descended on Don Zientara's Inner Ear Studio to record two tracks to be used on Dischord's *Flex Your Head* compilation and our first record, the *Legless Bull* EP. We were four smart-ass suburban teenagers on a mission to mock popular culture at top speed in the most stripped-down bare-bones way possible. No subject was too sacred to be off-limits. We skewered politicians, televangelists, silly fashion trends, people who think they're cooler than everyone else, and rock and roll itself.

When I say we descended on the studio, I mean it literally, since Inner Ear was the basement of Don's house at that time. We loaded our equipment in through the kitchen and made our way down the stairs to set up in the basement's main room. Our friend (and future Government bassist) Rob Moss came with us to help out with equipment. Besides the main room, there were a makeshift vocal booth and control room. The control room was pretty small, little more than a large walk-in closet. It contained the mixing board, two tape machines, and outboard gear. I don't remember the control room even having a window to the main room like recording studios normally have.

Because we were recording for Dischord, and Don had already recorded the first three Dischord releases, Ian MacKaye wanted us to record with Don as well. It turned out to be a good combination despite the limitations of the studio space and the gear that Don had at the time. Although Don seemed like an "old guy" to us teenagers, he was probably in his upper twenties or early thirties at most. Despite the age difference, Don put us all at ease right away, and we were pleasantly surprised at how open he was to helping us achieve what we were after. He encouraged us to go with some of our sillier ideas like the incidental vocal intros to "Rock and Roll Bullshit" and "Cowboy Fashion." He also suggested we do the gang vocals for the "Hey hey hey hey!" part on "Hey Ronnie," for which we all crowded around a single microphone in the vocal booth.

Marc Alberstadt, John Barry, and myself cut the instrumental tracks live, while John Stabb did a scratch vocal for reference. I don't remember us doing very many takes for any of the songs—one to three at most. There was no double-tracking or overdubbing. Track space was limited and our mindset was to keep things as real as possible. After the instrumental tracks were cut, Stabb recorded the final versions of the vocals, and finally we cut the incidental vocal intros and gang vocals. Rob's voice can be heard in the intro and at the end of "Cowboy Fashion" ("Moooo!"). After listening to the record again, I'm pretty sure I'm hearing Ian's voice in the intro of that song as well, saying, "C'mon, boy."

We came back to the studio on a second day to do the mixes. Ian was there as well to supervise the proceedings. The mixing was fairly straightforward until we got to "Sheer Terror." Stabb felt it needed something extra to make the song creepier in a campy sort of way. Don suggested that he could add some effects to the vocal to make this happen. The rest of us were skeptical, to say the least. Special effects on vocals?! We wouldn't be able to do that live, and it doesn't seem very punk rock! In the end, Don, with Stabb on his side, persuaded us to at least give it a try. I'm not exactly sure what combination of effects he used—delay? chorus? pitch shifting?—but when he played back the end result, we were convinced. Stabb's voice sounded like something from a B horror movie, and even though we wouldn't be able to recreate the effect live, it stayed that way for the record. After we decided that the vocal effect on "Sheer Terror" was okay, we gave Don and John a little more leeway, hence the slowed-down voice at the end of "I'm James Dean."

Although forty years have passed and my memory is hazy, I do remember how excited we were to actually be making a record, and how relieved we were that Don was easy to work with. Don's contributions were a crucial part of making *Legless Bull* and our tracks on *Flex Your Head* what they are.

John Barry

Government Issue

I remember walking into a tiny studio, I think it was a basement or the first floor. I had no idea what a recording studio was. Don was the operator; Ian was keeping it real. I just followed instructions: we were in a line of teeny punks being processed for posterity, so we had to get it done. Entitlement or high expectations never entered the mix. My pretzel-neck SG wasn't staying in tune, so someone from Minor Threat gave me a Les Paul. I think the session lasted about an hour at most. Calling it a session would be a stretch. It was like posing for a photo. We were back on the street before we had enough time to ruin it. I didn't make the production session, but when I listened to the first demo, I was surprised. Z had given us a nasty, jangly edge that captured our vibe really well. Inner Ear didn't try to turn us into anything we weren't; they didn't even let us try to turn ourselves into anything we weren't. Minor Threat was airtight; we were like a cat caught in a blender operating at top speed. That captured us perfectly, probably more perfectly than I wanted it to at the time. Forty years down the road, I don't think of Inner Ear in terms of a final product, just as a place where things were happening in real time.

Danny Ingram

Youth Brigade - Dot Dash

December 1, 2021, marked the fortieth anniversary of Youth Brigade's *Possible* EP. We recorded two sessions at Inner Ear—the output of which was used for the EP, plus a few songs on *Flex Your Head*. Youth Brigade was my second band, but this was my first time in a studio. Consequently, I had no appreciation for what it took to get from the basement to a finished product.

In the forty years since I first stepped foot into Don's, I've played in more than fifteen bands and recorded in more than a dozen studios. In 1993, I was in a short-lived band with John Stabb called Emma Peel. For me, it was a return to Inner Ear for the first time in twenty-three years. The thing I remember most is John's antics. Don had a small "room" to record vocals that looked like a converted shower stall. John spent hours in that stall riffing a stream-of-consciousness comedy routine (before actually singing). When I listen to that record, that is what I'm drawn back to: the people involved and the fun we had making it.

By 2018, my current band, Dot Dash, had already recorded five records for the Beautiful Music label. For our sixth, *Proto Retro*, we chose Inner Ear. This was coming full circle for me—and I was caught up in a wave of nostalgia as I took in all the records affixed to the walls that included so many of my friends and former bandmates.

Dot Dash are an efficient outfit and follow the same routine for each session: Load in Friday night. Record basic tracks Saturday and Sunday, usually in one take for bassist Hunter Bennet and myself. Then singer/guitarist Terry Banks does guitars on Sunday and vocals on Monday. Our talented friend Geoff Sanoff was at the helm as producer. He and engineer Eamonn Aiken did a great job making us feel relaxed throughout, and this is critical. All elements came together: creativity on both sides of the glass, working with people you trust, in an environment that makes you feel at home. The band, producer, and studio were all in sync. It not only captured the moment, it enhanced our vision of how it should sound. It was the last chance I had to record at Inner Ear, and I'm glad it ended on such a high note.

Chris Stover

Void

I remember arriving at Inner Ear and trying to figure out whether it was a real live studio or a kid's playroom. We had gone to another studio for a recording session. It was professional. Inner Ear was more our speed. With the help of Ian, Don, and Bert [Queiroz], the setup really let our creative juices flow. More like juices blowing out. Can we make the guitar squeal louder? "Sure," Don would say, and push it to ear-splitting level. The best was when we locked John in the shower stall for the song "Explode." He was not happy and I think the song reflected that.

Ivor Hanson

Faith - Embrace - Manifesto

Although Manifesto recorded in the "new" Inner Ear (the one that's actually been around for over thirty years), I really consider Inner Ear to be Don's basement since that's where Faith and Embrace recorded their albums.

In that studio, built into the wall that separated the control room from the recording room was a small window, as in, a square that was maybe twelve inches by twelve inches or smaller. And placed within that small window was a plastic figure—a dinosaur, perhaps? Maybe even a palm tree? And little lights too?—giving the window the feel of an empty aquarium.

I mention the dinosaur-in-the-window-in-the-studio-wall since it epitomizes Don Zientara for me: a sense of fun within the work.

For even though the bands were all there to do the serious work of laying down songs—and for me, as the drummer, that meant, say, not dropping a drumstick, or speeding up the songs, or going into a chorus with a cymbal crash too soon; those sorts of screw-ups—Don took the edge off what could easily be an intimidating situation.

I'd hear his engaging, encouraging voice come in though the headphones as we sorted out the snare sound, the bass drum sound, the cymbals' sounds, or after a take of a song, and know that everything was going great or going to be great.

He'd make suggestions; he'd make jokes; he made the records happen. Thanks, Don!

Alec MacKaye

Faith - Ignition - Hammered Hulls

Hanging out with Lungfish during the *Love Is Love* taping, watching the levels on the sound board. Vertical rows of green glowing dots driven by sound, rising up and falling back, to the rhythm of "Peace Mountains of Peace."

The walls of the studio, covered with original drawings, prints, and paintings by people I knew, and many others I didn't. Tempera paint on kraft paper—scenery made by little kids for a classroom play. It was inspiring to be surrounded by people's direct creative output, rather than slick posters advertising tech equipment or tidy, framed awards on plain walls. Puzzles and toys scattered on the tables, always within reach to open mind traps that sometimes cropped up while navigating a song.

More than the setting, though, the real tone-setter was the engineer. Wherever Don is, is where Inner Ear is. It takes a certain type of person to stay open-minded while artists settle into the engine room/control room and try to get somewhere, typically not fully knowing the destination until it arrives. Don is the type of artist who understands how to make the tools work for the maker, rather than telling the maker to work for the tools. This is a gift more than a skill. It takes an imaginative, fearless, and industrious mind to resist lecturing a juvenile-delinquent rocker to turn down his overdriven, clapped-out Fender Twin that is bleeding through the drum mics. Don might just say: "Do you want to let it bleed?"

I recorded a number of records at Inner Ear. Starting in 1982 in Don's house, spanning forty years until the last months of its existence in the building on Oakland Street at Four Mile Run. I loved the space. It was the perfect balance of comfortable and intentional. Making a record there is like going on a submarine mission. You stop at the co-op or convenience store, stock up on supplies for the trip, then hunker down in the engine room for entire days and nights, fully immersed in your craft.

Franz Stahl

Scream

Nothing was more life-changing to my budding musical endeavors than to go into a real studio for the first time, and to record Scream's first record. My only regret is that we did not take any pictures or video of our first time there, at least not until Scream came back to Inner Ear the first week of September 2021 to record what is now the LAST full record to be recorded there. My wife documented the entire experience on film, video, and photos, while she and associates also conducted twenty-one interviews about the whole project, Inner Ear, and Don, and his life at the helm of one of the most important studios in the DMV area. It was an historic event to say the least, and quite the undertaking by both band, guest musicians, and the documentarians, and of course Ian and Don.

I was an adolescent upstart with limited studio experience, and even more limited musicianship, when we found ourselves about to record twenty-one fast blazing punk rock songs in the basement of this not-well-known studio. I have vague memories of the actual basement aside from the this little window in a room that was the control room in the boiler room part, which they—Don and Ian—could peer through to the main part of the basement room where the band

Scream *DC Special* recording session in the summer of 2021, celebrating forty years of the band's musical journey and inviting friends from the DC community to collaborate. TOP LEFT: (left to right) Ian MacKaye, Franz Stahl, and Don Zientara. Photo by Sal Owen. BOTTOM LEFT: (left to right) Don and Skeeter Thompson. Photo by Sal Owen. TOP RIGHT: Pete Stahl. Photo by Sal Owen. MIDDLE RIGHT: (left to right) Franz Stahl and Don. Photo by Farrah Skeiky. BOTTOM RIGHT: (left to right) Franz Stahl, Joe Lally, and Mark Cisneros. Photo by Sal Owen.

set up and tracked. The small built-in shelves I remember with toys and assorted collectibles around the room. I had expected to meet this typical know-it-all studio engineer who would belittle my incompetence with regard to our music and my playing. It was nothing like that at all. He was tall, soft spoken, and extremely patient, and you could tell it was pure joy for him to be recording, guiding, and providing, and he extended this too to the band. His friendliness had a lasting affect on all of us, an experience I will never forget. For all this past to come full circle in our most recent visit makes it all the more special. I had not been back in years, and upon my return I found the exact same person, slightly older, but probably even more patient and affable. I think myself, as well as him, in this situation brought on much retrospection of the years, the ending of it all, and Don once again recording our band. I cannot think of a finer gentle musical soul than Don.

VA's own George Martin. I do hope it is not years again that separate us and another hang with this gentleman.

Pete Stahl

Scream

Rather than creativity being compromised in the studio, it's an opportunity for it to grow. If you're lucky enough to have the chance to record your music in a studio, it becomes the next step in a creative process. When you enter, all of a sudden you have a team with a producer and engineer to assist you in realizing the vision of a song or an album, which is why Inner Ear is and was so important to us and the DC-area music scene. We learned our shit there and had a space to blossom in.

We were fortunate to be befriended by the bassist Jefferson Rogers of the band the Laymen. I can't recall the exact details, but I think we played a show together at Poseurs in Georgetown and he then brought us into Inner Ear to record with him and Don. It was surreal just to be in a recording studio to begin with, but the original Inner Ear was in a house that was located on the same street my brother and I grew up on years before. The studio was just a few doors down and on the same side of the street as our old duplex. The layout of Don's basement was the same as our basement—which was my bedroom, with its blacklight posters and the stereo we'd listen to local radio and records on while stoned, years before we made the step to form a band.

So recording at Don's was like returning to the womb, and Inner Ear became our studio home. The demo we did with Jefferson and Don got us our first gigs around town and we began to poke around to play regionally. The demo got us played on WHFS and reviewed by Howard Wuelfing in the local zine *Discords*. It got our foot in the door; subsequent recordings at Inner Ear continued our progression as a band. It was Don's patience and gentle guidance that allowed him to capture the energy of what we were—a young band playing in the basement. That is where we are from and what we wrote about on *Still Screaming* in the song "We're Fed Up." The basement is where we always return to. It's where we live in the sound that brings us back to life.

We learned from Don to just go for it and to not second guess ourselves. He helped us learn not to spend a lot of time trying to make it sound perfect. That is a real challenge in working within today's studio environment in the digital world. Trusting your gut allows you to take a chance.

Until recently, It had been over thirty years since we had recorded at Inner Ear. With our newest project, which we are calling *DC Special*, we could not tell the story we wanted to without Inner Ear being the headwaters from which the project would flow. Once again, Inner Ear is the place we came to tell our stories through local music history, to close out a chapter for a studio that helped shape our lives, and to write a new one that is truly special.

Anne Bonafede

Chalk Circle

Chalk Circle recorded a few songs in Don's basement studio about forty years ago—yikes! I remember feeling overwhelmed by all the recording and mixing gear. Don was really patient and took care to make sure we got the sound we wanted.

At some point, I wandered off from the process and picked up one of those See 'n Say toys where you pull a string to hear different animal sounds—Don had young kids at the time and their toys were scattered about. I liked the sounds and wanted to add them to the percussion, so that is what we did!

Specifically, the horse sound was mixed into the ending of one of the songs, and the result was just the chaotic, discordant sound we were going for.

And you definitely could not tell that it came from a toy!

David Fair

Half Japanese - CooCooRockinTime

I used to play in a band called Half Japanese. I absolutely loved being in the band and absolutely hated it as well. I loved hanging with people that I loved hanging with. I loved writing songs. I couldn't wait to get onstage. I was never even one ounce of nervous. But I hated playing in smoky bars and going to regular work with no sleep at all. I tried to quit the band when I turned thirty, but I was drawn back in by the enormous amount of fun. Eventually I came up with the idea that if I recorded with another band after Half Japanese, it would give me the separation needed to finally feel like I had left the original band. So I wrote a batch of songs for a new band called CooCooRockinTime. It actually had the same members as Half Japanese except that Jad was out of the country so he is not on it, and we added in Charles Brohawn from the Tinklers.

We booked up a few days to record in Don's basement. Don is among the sweetest people I have ever met. He knew all there was to know about recording and was so easy to work with. My band was an acquired taste but he never acted like we were recording anything but Grammy bait. He never interfered with anything that we were doing. He was there to make us feel comfortable and capture whatever we had to offer. He accomplished that as though he could've done it in his sleep. He knew what to do so thoroughly that it appeared effortless.

There was just one time that he made a suggestion to help us out. We had recorded a song called "Oldsmobile Girl Magnet 88." The music and original vocals were done live. Then it came time to add in some background vocals. This was a slow, ultra-romantic song that begged for some candy-sweet Jordanaires-style vocals. We sang like angels and nailed it on the first take.

Then Don's voice came over the speaker and announced, "Well, we'll have to take that again." I could barely believe my ears.

"What are you talking about? That was perfect."

"Well, I don't know," said Don, "I think we'd better go again."

I said, "It sounded good to me, we can just put it low in the mix."

Again Don's voice came from the next room: "You can't get it low enough in the mix."

So there you go. We knew Don knew his business, we did it over, and we put the second version low in the mix.

Don Fleming

Citizen 23 - The Velvet Monkeys - Half Japanese - Pea Soup

Thomas Edison built the first recording studio less than 150 years ago at his complex in West Orange, New Jersey. It was a huge advance in documenting music when wax cylinders made it possible to both capture and play back sound. Musicologists used this new technology in the field, capturing music where it occurred. These early song catchers did not bring singers into a studio to record their music, they went to where the music naturally occurred—at a public event, in a tavern, on a street corner, or in the musician's home. But mostly, starting with Edison's West Orange studio, musicians were required to come to a location where the recording equipment was set up. Studio recordings became more like formal portraits, rather than the snapshots captured by field recordings of performers at their own locations. Musicians, producers, and engineers have struggled ever since with striking a balance between a natural performance and the sterile effect that can happen with the process of recording in a studio. Inner Ear found that balance—documenting and nurturing the DC music scene during a rarefied time.

In 1980 I was in a band from Williamsburg, Virginia, called Citizen 23 that included Elaine Barnes, Steven Soles, and Susan Marquis. We often played at the Taj Mahal in Virginia Beach, and opened shows for the Slickee Boys and Insect Surfers at the Pub on the William & Mary campus. Susan moved to DC that May and started working for Skip Groff at Yesterday and Today, DJing at the 9:30 Club, became the Slickees's manager, and started booking shows for us in DC. Elaine, Steven, and I decided to make our break from the Tidewater scene, changed our name to the Velvet Monkeys, and moved into a small brick house on N. Powhatan Street in Falls Church, in the west end of Arlington.

Skip invited us to Inner Ear for our first session at the studio, which would result in recording six songs, including our two on the *Connected* compilation, "Shadow Box" and "Drive In." I had recorded at a couple of studios so was a bit surprised

Half Japanese

Stills from video by Margaret Bodde taken in 1987 while recording an as-yet-unreleased record. TOP LEFT: Jad Fair (front) and Don Fleming. TOP CENTER: Jad Fair (front) and Don Fleming. TOP RIGHT: Jad Fair. MIDDLE LEFT: Don Zientara (left) and Jay Spiegel. MIDDLE RIGHT: Don Zientara. BOTTOM LEFT: Jay Spiegel. BOTTOM RIGHT: tape machines.

when we pulled up to the Inner Ear address and it was a home in a quiet South Arlington neighborhood. We made the rookie mistake of knocking on the front door, but were soon carrying our gear down the steps into the basement, for the first of many times. We quickly fell in love with the place and working with Don. On that first session he had built a sweeping EQ filter with one knob that I used on my guitar during the mix for the chorus of "Favorite Day." It was the first of many times that I noted Don's passion for building DIY devices for recording and mixing. I loved the microphones he built for drummers to wear like a medallion. We found inspiration in Don's ideas, his passion for the process.

Over the next six years I recorded at Inner Ear with the Velvet Monkeys, Half Japanese, and Pea Soup. The crazier the project, the more Don seemed to embrace it. Many of the Half Japanese songs were improvisations to lyrics that Jad and David brought to the studio. We would do three or four takes, sometimes refining the arrangement, other times doing completely different music. Don never blinked. We had a limited amount of tape and would sometimes wipe over takes, but Don kept it all straight, calmly coming over the talkback, slating the next take, "'Nicole Told Me'—take two." If we showed up with our Dr. Rhythm drum machine, or three drummers, it was no problem, just be ready for Don to occasionally run into the studio from the control room between takes and make some quick adjustments.

We felt at home in this modest basement that looked like our own basement practice space a few miles away, but it really came down to Don's instinct to let things happen and capture them live and quickly. The Inner Ear sessions have great fidelity thanks to Don's innate skill as an engineer, but feel like field recordings, catching the essence of a broad range of fringe local musicians. His approach and temperament worked well with our various misfit bands, and we passed the word around to like-minded musicians looking for a safe and creative space to capture their sound.

We were always working toward the next session at Inner Ear to record our newest songs with Don. On the Half Japanese *Charmed Life* album, no producer is listed, the only credit is, *Recorded by Don Zientara*. I learned a great deal from watching Don at Inner Ear, which later influenced my work as a producer. He let bands be themselves, embraced spontaneity, and never let the studio technology interrupt the flow of the sessions.

In many ways we are still in the infancy of the era of recorded sound, with digital recording being the latest technological twist. Edison's mono audio track has evolved to seemingly infinite tracks on a laptop, and users of digital recording are further lulled into creating smoothed-out formal portraits. Don's discography from Inner Ear stands as a vital example of the opposite, capturing a snapshot of the unbridled energy of each group of musicians. We were very fortunate to have Inner Ear, and the innovative spirit of Don Zientara, to catch all of these songs.

Howard Wuelfing

The Nurses - Half Japanese

My first meeting with Don Zientara was at his home in South Arlington. I'd answered a Wanted ad in the *Unicorn Times* (most likely) seeking musicians and citing the Yardbirds, the Who, and Roxy Music as reference points. This was the Look, and we rehearsed on Columbia Road in the basement of a row house being rehabbed by the guitar player Robert Goldstein. The group mainly played relatively unusual covers for the day (and eventually one original song). We needed a tape to solicit gigs with and Robert knew a guy from the AV department at the National Gallery he'd played with in a folk rock outfit called Ravenstone who he talked into recording us.

We trucked our gear out to South Arlington, brought it around back, in through the kitchen door, and down the stairs to Don's daughter's playroom. We moved toys out of the way and set up. Don had cut a hole in the wall between the playroom and boiler room to run the mic cords through. Since we'd rehearsed enough to play out, we simply ran through the set (maybe we did some songs twice), and that was that.

About a year later, we'd moved to South Arlington and I'd formed a trio called the Nurses (a tribute to my mom—also, it intentionally didn't conform with the emerging punk style dictating that names ought to be shocking), and following the example of the Slickee Boys (who I'd recently left amicably) we decided to record a single and checked in with Don, who was indeed still recording bands in what was now called Studio Z.

The studio was still in the playroom but now the control room was upstairs in a little study and there was a bit more gear. Sessions at Studio Z were always fun. The atmosphere was always relaxed and informal, the rates were always reasonable (it could have been that you'd pay per session and not by the hour), and we'd normally track, overdub, and mix two songs in one session. Don always had excellent ideas for translating a rough idea into a recording strategy. In particular I recall being deep in an Al Green jag and wanting to replicate the drum sound of the Hi Rhythm Section and Don suggesting we detune the floor tom until it had that same thumpy bounce.

He also loved to trot out new gear and recording tricks and was surprisingly open to abusing them to get novel results. When we were mixing the final Nurses single, he had recently purchased a harmonizer (I think), a device that'd add a harmony line to a vocal or instrumental line. And instantly the question arose: what'd happen if you turned on the effect and then the knob? And this wonderful weird, phased sound emerged, which wound up inspiring an extended "dance mix" of said track as well as a lovely chorused guitar solo achieved using the effect as intended. I had a number of great experiences working at Don's: cutting the Reind Dears Christmas single with members of the Slickees and Pin-Ups helping out the Nurses; being jammed in that basement in the middle of summer with a dozen other players for Half Japanese sessions.

It was always fun, always relaxed, and usually yielded surprising results thanks to Don.

Mark Jickling

Half Japanese

Half Japanese recorded an album at Inner Ear every year from 1982 to 1987. That was in the Ivy Street basement, before Shirlington. The group was normally five or six people, but when we went to record we wanted a "big band" sound. So we would march in with two or three drummers, a horn section, and half a dozen guitarists. We barely fit in the room; it was definitely elbow to elbow. Without any fuss, Don would mic everything up, and give us all headphones. We played at our normal stage volume, which was amps on ten.

Somehow, not only did the recordings sound good, but Don was able to get enough separation that we could mix all the tracks. At the time, this seemed normal. But having recorded in other places over the years since, I now realize that normal producers and engineers would just freak out over what we wanted to do, and try to steer us to overdubbing or reasonable room volumes. Or else throw up their hands, press "record," and come out with a mess of hiss and roar. Don was able to capture the musical qualities we had, along with the noise.

I don't think there's a technical term for this gift of Don's: to take whatever comes through the door, and, seemingly without effort, make it sound as good as it's ever going to sound, all the while radiating such good humor that if the musicians aren't swept up in the joy of making music, they need to be in another line of work.

Rob Kennedy

Chumps - Half Japanese - The Velvet Monkeys

Despite having some really fun sessions at Inner Ear with the Chumps, the session I remember best is the Half Japanese big band session. This was in the "old" Inner Ear. The "room" was about ten feet by twelve feet and chock-full of mics and amps. Into that space we fit Jad and David Fair and the rest of the current version of Half Jap—Ruki and John Dreyfuss, Lana Zabko, and Mark Jickling. Both Workdogs were there. Don and Rummy from the Velvet Monkeys. A couple Orthotonics came up from Richmond. And—oh yeah, Eugene Chadbourne and his rake. Two drum kits! You couldn't turn ten degrees without whacking someone with your instrument. Somehow or other Don managed to mic this mess and make it sound coherent. In one day this crew recorded something like twenty-four songs! Don never lost his cool for one minute. An awesome session.

Jay Spiegel aka The Rummager

The Velvet Monkeys - Half Japanese

I did several sessions in the early to mid '80s at the original Inner Ear Studio. Bands recording were the Velvet Monkeys, Half Japanese, Crippled Pilgrims, and Pea Soup. The most memorable session for me was a Half Japanese session for

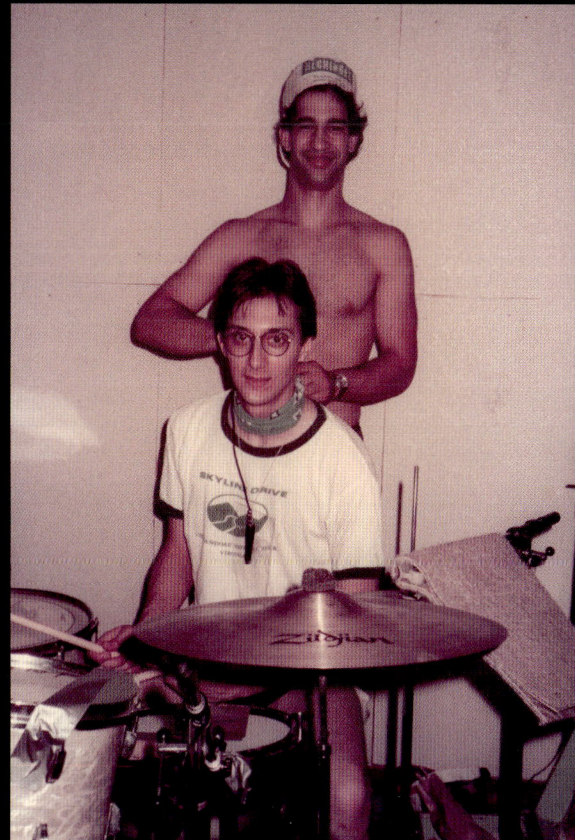

Jay Spiegel (drums) and Joey Picuri. A Velvet Monkeys session, circa 1983. Photo courtesy of Joey Picuri.

the album *Charmed Life*. Recording with Half Japanese meant a lot of personnel, six to eight, and doing most everything live in one take. I remember there was stuff everywhere. Between the band members, all our instruments and amps, recording mics and cords, you couldn't even see the floor. Once you had your spot you didn't move too much. This was when I especially liked playing drums since I had a wall around me and could just hang behind the kit. It was in the summer so it got pretty hot and sweaty. During breaks we'd all pile outside and hang in Don's backyard. Juanita [Don's wife] would usually come out to say hi and their daughters would come out to play some games with us. It was a great time. My other memory is how easy Don was to work with. There was never any pressure to get the take right. Just gentle advice on how to make the recording better.

Jason Carmer

9353 - Double-O

[Interview and transcription by Jason's fifteen-year-old son Nico.]

When I was fifteen, one of my friends told me about a band called Double-O who needed a new guitar player.

At the time it was my dream to be in a punk band, so I decided to try out. I will be honest, I wasn't that good, but they were impressed. Anyway, I got the gig.

We ended up playing lots of shows and I was still fifteen, so it was awesome. Eventually we decided to make a record. We booked hours at Inner Ear Studio, because at that time that's where popular records were done. I was nervous because I didn't know what it would be like. I thought it would be something in between a dentist and an airport terminal. I remember practicing in my room all the time to prepare.

The day comes to go to the studio and I'm pretty nervous. We pulled up to a brick house and now I'm imagining some Dr. Evil lair below the house. Don answered the door and he was super friendly. He brought us down to his basement and it was basically a den. We started to set up our stuff and I had to move some kids toys to make room for my amp. It was definitely different than what I thought it would be.

He had the original tapes of the bands he recorded and I thought it was so cool. Don was really able to make us comfortable. He told us to not worry about making mistakes and play the song like you mean it. I think we only played each song like once or twice, because we really didn't mess up.

When we listened to what we recorded, it felt cool because I hadn't listened to anything I played before come out of a speaker worth more than twenty dollars. I think that was the moment I realized that this is what I wanted to do. It was a real wake-up moment.

At that time, I didn't relate to anyone at my school. Honestly, I wasn't that social at all. This experience made me feel I was really a part of something. It was a big moment for me to walk into Don's studio and see the way he was so engaged and helping us. When you're making music, there is an insecurity that comes with exposing yourself, and Don was so good at making you believe in yourself. Those experiences in Don's studio put me on the path that I'm on today and I'm so grateful for the opportunity to go there.

Dan Joseph

9353 - The Crippled Pilgrims - Troubled Gardens

The first time I ever set foot in a recording studio was in early 1983, at Inner Ear. I was sixteen, and my high school friend Jason's band was recording a four-song demo. The band, 9353, which had only existed for a short time, had been using a drum machine in place of a drummer, and wanted a few live percussion accents added to their demo tracks. Jason had asked if I was interested in helping, and I naturally agreed. Without any rehearsal I showed up at Don's house in Arlington with parts of my drum kit—high-hat, snare, cymbals, Rototoms—and we began in earnest down in Don's basement.

I remember things being pretty cramped in the studio, with a low ceiling and not much light. I think most of the other tracks had already been done before I arrived, and I'm pretty sure all three band members were there, and I remember being pretty terrified. Not only had I never been in a studio before, I had never really been in a proper band either. Fortunately, Don was a natural director and producer. His obvious enthusiasm and bright personality helped ease my anxiety, and I remember him literally coaching me when to hit, how to hit, what to hit . . . "Great job!"

That first session was a success, and within weeks I had become a full member of 9353 and was rehearsing with the group. Soon we were back at Inner Ear as a four-piece, recording another batch of songs. These later sessions were more involved, and more difficult, but again Don kept us on track and helped steer us in the right direction. By the end of the second round of sessions, 9353 had recorded a whopping twelve songs!

9353 would later record at other studios, never returning to Inner Ear. That was a mistake, and in retrospect, our recordings at Don's were far and away the best recordings we made, and it remains a minor tragedy that the masters from those sessions mysteriously disappeared.

Later in the '80s I returned to Inner Ear to record a project I was then doing with cellist Rogelio Maxwell. We worked primarily with Geoff Turner, who I think was then a part-time engineer at the studio. Nonetheless, Don came downstairs and peeked in on our sessions a few times, offering impressions and encouragement, helping to make these sessions a success too. I am very grateful for the good fortune of having recorded at Inner Ear and working with Don Z., the legend.

Dug E. Bird (Birdzell)

Beefeater - Fidelity Jones

In February of 1985, Beefeater went to Inner Ear Studio to record *Plays for Lovers*, and the song "Wars in Space," which was released on WGNS Records' *Alive and Kicking* compilation.

We had a good vibe in practice and we'd played about six shows. We were used to playing our songs pretty intensely, really focusing on each other for the hard parts and keeping breaks between songs super short. We all felt really positive and ready for a good studio session. We loaded in, got set up, got our basic sounds, then took a quick break to get food. I went to Mario's Pizza and got a scrambled egg sub with marinara sauce and a Coke.

We did all the basic tracks that night. Fifteen songs, all first takes, all live in the studio: guitar, drums, and bass. Don and

Ian provided lots of good humor and encouragement to keep us in the moment and moving forward. We band members had each other's backs throughout the session. That made a big difference to me, especially when I kicked off "Song for Lucky." In the end, recording felt a lot like playing a show. The biggest difference to me was wearing headphones.

We were all unified with our music. We had the right amount of technology for recording. Nothing overwhelming. Don and Ian encouraged us to stay true to ourselves. I felt no need to hold the line on messing around with studio effects and messing up our songs. Freak (Fred Smith) didn't even overdub guitar solos.

At the end of the night I thanked Ian. I felt like we had really succeeded in documenting our music and ourselves in that moment.

Bruce Taylor

Beefeater - Shock Treatment - Visigoths - Hate from Ignorance

We were recording our 1988 demo for Shock Treatment, an original hard rock band I had at the time, at Inner Ear Studio. We played a crude recording from one of our practices to give Don a feel for the sound we were going for. To my surprise, he said, "Those drums almost sound like Rototoms . . . only deeper." I had taken old Roto drums and added drum shells to them . . . and he picked out that subtle nuance . . . from a crappy recording. I was dumbfounded.

We were recording our 1989 self-released album for Visigoths, a doom/punk band I had at the time, at Inner Ear Studio. We laid down the tracks and were doing mix-down and I asked Don for a sample of an anvil to insert in the rhythm track. He said, "I don't have a bunch of samples lying around, but I'll see what I can do." He found a gold railroad spike in his house and we used a triangle striker to sound it and it turned out to be a darn good "anvil" sound on the record!

I remember that in 1982 I was recording at Inner Ear for the *Mixed Nuts Don't Crack* compilation with my band Hate from Ignorance. I was trying to use an analog drum synth for the recording. Don suggested some techniques and I ended up running the drum pad white noise generator through a Morley-powered wah-wah pedal and came up with a perfect "windstorm" effect for the background intro of one of our songs. Always the innovator!!!

Wow, the session with Beefeater at Inner Ear was amazing. Don had everything so dialed in and had a perfect environment for recording. We ended up doing all the songs in one take. Ian (aka Gumbo MacKaye) and Don worked their magic in the studio for mix-down and ended up with one of the most amazing albums I've ever heard. The music industry is losing an icon in the business and I feel blessed to have been a small part of that experience.

Dante Ferrando

Iron Cross - Gray Matter - Ignition

The thing I loved the most about the Gray Matter and Ignition sessions we did at Inner Ear was Don's understanding of the stresses of recording, and his calming style. The sessions were short, with just a few days to record and mix a record.

Beefeater

Beefeater's 1986 *House Burning Down* recording session with guests. TOP LEFT: Tomas Squip. TOP RIGHT: Fred Smith. MIDDLE LEFT: Dug E. Bird. MIDDLE CENTER: Kenny Craun. MIDDLE RIGHT: Amy Pickering. BOTTOM LEFT: Alec MacKaye. BOTTOM RIGHT: Don Zientara. Photos by Tomas Squip.

The songs were sometimes not fully finished, and the members of those bands, myself included, were very high-strung people who were trying to turn a lot of very raw emotion into music and get it on tape fast. Don thought about the small details that would keep things running smooth, like strangely weak coffee so bands wouldn't get too amped up, his vast collection of fidget toys, and timely suggestions for food breaks when he noticed bands getting too stressed or cranky.

When Gray Matter was recording *Head*, we explained to Don that we wanted to do a very long backing track that was basically the four band members with our friends Jon K. and Tomas, in a room having a screaming cathartic freakout as the song played. As soon as he understood what we were trying to do, he said, "I think I have a red light bulb around here somewhere," and with that as the only light in the room, he managed to set the mood up perfectly.

As weird as things got, Don never flinched.

Mark Haggerty

Iron Cross - Gray Matter - Three

The first time I was at Don's was at the studio in the basement of his house recording the *Food for Thought* LP with Gray Matter, when we were all in high school.

The control room was cozy, warm from the tube lights on top of the homemade console that the gallery of reel-to-reel tapes that was the museum of DC punk history was behind: Bad Brains, Teen Idles, SOA, Minor Threat, and so many more. Definitely a certain good creative pressure to do the right thing and make something good within these walls. Don was so nice. Cheerful, funny, kind, a surfer guy rather than a rock dude, tan and in flip-flops, with a cup of coffee.

He liked Gray Matter, our sense of humor was comfortable, and it was really fun. Besides Ian and Bert [Queiroz] producing and keeping us on track, Skeeter [Thompson] and Molly [Burnham] stopped by for whatever reason and ended up singing background vocals, as well as Amy [Pickering], who we planned on asking.

I kinda started to understand what Don had created in his basement: his kids cruised around upstairs, and we set up our gear around all their stuffed animals and toys, we made coffee and tea in the kitchen, and said hi to his family. It was, within practical reason, a place you could be yourself, and Don was into it. I think we felt a kinship with him and I was so proud to record there and be a witness to the engine that is Inner Ear Studio.

Andy Charneco

Fidelity Jones - Cigarbox Planetarium

Fidelity Jones entered Inner Ear Studio in 1988 or 1989 to record *Piltdown Lad*. I remember it like it was only thirty-three years ago.

I'd already known Don and his studio for over ten years, and I'm pretty sure Dug, Jerry, and Onam [Tomas] had worked

Three

Three, *Dark Days Coming* session, 1987. TOP LEFT: Jeff Nelson. Photo by Geoff Turner. BOTTOM LEFT: (left to right) Geoff Turner, Don Zientara, and Mark Haggerty. Photo by Jeff Nelson. RIGHT: (left to right) Geoff Turner, Mark Haggerty, and Steve Niles. Photo by Jeff Nelson.

with him before. We had a tour on the horizon and wanted to get a record of where we were at at the time. We didn't have many songs ready to go so we put out the recordings as a six-song EP.

At that point Don had the studio in the basement of his house. When I first met Don, the control room was upstairs in the sunroom, which meant if you wanted to hear the playback, you had to go up the stairs, through the living room, and into the sunroom, only to discover that you needed to go back and do it all again. When Fidelity Jones recorded there, the control room was in the basement, right next to the studio.

The band decided early on that we wanted the basic tracks to be done live and together, with only the vocals and minimal sundry percussion to be overdubbed. Our *Sgt. Pepper* could wait. We recorded everything in one day, mixed everything on another day, and then determined that the end result was lacking, so went in on a third day to do the final mix. Onam came up with the title, as he was the only paleoanthropologist in the band. We had a great time and all of us felt comfortable with Don and his rooms.

Anyway, I'm looking forward to the eventual reappraisal and multidisc box set. Maybe it will include the mystery first mix! My memories here—seeming as clear as a bell now—are probably 95 percent false.

One Beyond Zebra (later in the band Betty). Left to right: Amy Ziff, Elizabeth Ziff, Alyson Palmer, and Andy Charneco, 1984. Photo courtesy of Don Zientara.

Shawn Brown

Dag Nasty - Swiz - Red Hare

Halloween, 1985. It was the first time Dag had recorded and the first time I personally had ever recorded. A small studio operated out of a house in Arlington. The weight felt almost unbearable to my eighteen-year-old self. Should I try to relax or just scream my head off and punk out?? Unfamiliar territory soon became familiar.

A balance of raw power and technical finesse is what I think Inner Ear brought to the music. Don and the studio were integral in shaping a unique local sound. He was able to capture a live-show essence in the recordings. They have that kind of feel to them.

Legends were born there.

I am thankful to have had the pleasure of recording with Don over the years, as well as for all that the music made at Inner Ear has taught me and still does. I am honored to be a part of that legacy.

Colin Sears

Dag Nasty

Depending on how you count, I was fortunate to have recorded eight to ten full-length releases at Inner Ear from 1983 until 2015 when Dag Nasty recorded our last 7" for Dischord. I was also lucky enough to have gotten a chance to record at both the original basement Inner Ear as well as the totally pro updated space that was built out afterward and has only recently shuttered.

By the time I recorded at Inner Ear with Dag Nasty in 1985, I recognized how special the studio was and how lucky I was to get the chance to record there. Although I moved away from the DC area in 1987, I returned to Inner Ear to record with several other bands over the years (as well as return with Dag Nasty for various sessions).

I feel that Don Z. created a comfortable space that didn't subtract from the character of the music but rather enhanced it. This helped capture and document the music that the bands I was part of created together in the basement and refined onstage (sometimes, but not often enough—the first few Dag Nasty LPs being the exception here). The ambiance Don created in the new space was like a warm blanket or a cozy toddler's room (despite its spaciousness).

Don was adept at pushing technology to its boundaries in order to emulate the sound and the soul of a basement or the 9:30 Club stage, etc. Don was also always willing to share the truth about parts of our songs that didn't work and performances that were underwhelming or lackluster. Don would also highlight what really DID work with our songs and how we might push ourselves just a bit more to get that perfect performance (or rewrite the bridge). Ultimately, working with Don at Inner Ear made the task of the performer a bit tougher, but the rewards and payback were always worth it.

I remember going to record *Wig Out at Denkos* with Don and I think I played him an overproduced U2 song from their most recent release and said: "We want the snare drum to sound like this." Don replied, "Then you need to write songs like that (and maybe buy a better snare)."

Dag Nasty, *Cold Heart* session, 2015. TOP LEFT: (left to right) Roger Marbury, Shawn Brown, Don, Ian MacKaye, and Brian Baker. TOP RIGHT: (left to right) Ian MacKaye, Don Zientara, Brian Baker, and Colin Sears. MIDDLE LEFT: (left to right) Ian MacKaye, Don Zientara, Brian Baker, Colin Sears, Roger Marbury, and Shawn Brown. MIDDLE RIGHT: Ian MacKaye at the mixer, Brian Baker (left) and Roger Marbury behind the glass. BOTTOM: Dag Nasty outside Inner Ear (left to right) Shawn Brown, Brian Baker, Roger Marbury, and Colin Sears. Photos by Michelle C. Roberts.

Nick Pellicciotto

At Wit's End - Edsel - New Wet Kojak

When I was in high school in Maryland, me and three friends—John England, Nick MacIntosh, and Elias Anthan—formed a band called At Wit's End. We started writing songs inspired by the local DC-area punk bands we'd seen at the all-ages shows we started going to around 1986, promoted mainly by the organization Positive Force.

After sharing a few bills with some of our idols and getting a chance to talk to them about how to do a band, we learned that we could just call Don and book some time at Inner Ear, which we did in the winter of 1987. It amazed us that we could record in the same studio that the bands we revered recorded—bands like Rites of Spring, Bad Brains, and Minor Threat.

We wanted some of that "fairy dust" that peppered our favorite records to rub off on us. I'm not sure if it did, but the experience of recording at Inner Ear was fun and inspiring. And the reason for that was Don Zientara.

We thought of ourselves as suburban nobodies, but Don treated us with so much respect and made us feel so comfortable that we didn't really feel self-consciousness at all. My mom drove us over there, and instead of leaving, Don invited her in to the control room to hang out for a bit. They totally hit it off, chatting and laughing while we set up. Don seemed to instinctively know how to do just the right thing to make people relax.

The studio was really cozy and had very warm lighting, so it felt a bit like being on a submarine, with Don as the amiable captain. He never really told us if a take or whatever was good or bad, but just gently nudged us in the right direction. And even when we were on our third or fourth take of a song, he always said "take one" into the talkback mic before hitting the record button. I must say, the first time he said it, I felt like I had died and gone to heaven—I had heard that voice say "take one" on countless records I loved. I couldn't believe it was happening to me in real life.

We ended up recording a six-song demo tape that took two days to finish.

It wasn't until I'd done other recording sessions in other studios that I realized how special it was to work with Don. And only in retrospect have I realized how fundamental that particular recording session was on determining the direction of my life.

Fire Party interviewed by Stefanie Williams

September 2021

Stefanie Williams: What was it like recording at Inner Ear?

Natalie Avery: It was so mythical to me. It was a basement in a house in Arlington. There were a lot of times that I would be like, *Oh my god, I can't believe that I'm here in this place.* That's where the studio was for our first two records. Yeah, I mean, until when, Amy, did he move? Like that was in the mid '90s.

Amy Pickering: Yeah, for sure. Actually, I was over at his house the other day and the back deck and all of that is totally something different.

Williams: What was it like to record with Don?

Avery: So nice and funny.

Pickering: Dry, a little calm. He's like, "Let's listen to that." Every time. And if you ask his opinion, you pretty much always want to take his suggestion. He's pretty much always right.

Kate Samworth: He's got a very incredible way of making you feel totally comfortable. "Disarming" I guess is the word. He's super easy to be around and to work with and I think I was super intimidated going into that studio because all of it was so new, and it was like now we're gonna put everything down, there's no denying what people heard, and he makes you feel like you belong there. Even if you're feeling like a total beginner, he's like, "No, of course you should be recording this."

Avery: I remember I did some guitar overdubs that I'd never done before. I'd written them the night before in my room and it was kind of nerve-racking going to the studio because you feel really on the spot. When the whole band is recording you're just like recording, but it's a little more intricate when you're playing along with yourself and trying to add guitar overdubs. I was struggling a little because I was so nervous and I just remember him totally putting me at ease. I can imagine it being kind of annoying when you have somebody playing the same thing over and over again and not getting it, but he would just take it in stride. I mean, I don't know how he actually felt, but that's what I think we mean by welcoming.

Pickering: And also, intensely patient. We're gonna do your fifty-fifth take. That's no problem, here we go. He is unbelievable.

Williams: You touched on this a little bit, Natalie, but what was Fire Party's creative process when making music?

Avery: Well, in the beginning, I think either Kate or I would bring a song. When we first started I had some songs that I had written that nobody had played to before. I would come to practice and be like, "Hey, here's a song," and then everybody would write to it and then we would talk about it and hash it out. Sometimes it would be a full song, sometimes it would be just a part, and then sometimes Kate would bring a part and I would add to it. There was a lot of talking about the songs and talking about the part. I remember "Engine" and I think Kate just sort of accidentally played. I remember it felt like it was just spontaneous playing those notes and then it sort of emerged into a song. That's my memory of the process. And one thing is we had guitar amp, bass amp, and drums. But Amy kind of sang to herself, we didn't have a PA. So we really didn't hear Amy and her vocals until we went to the studio. I mean, we kind of heard when we were playing live, but it's so different when you play live versus when you hear it in the moment when you're sitting there like, *Whoa, wow.*

Samworth: It's so insane that we didn't just figure out how to buy a little PA. I mean, geez, I'm sorry, but what a disadvantage!

Pickering: It kind of gave me time to take it in and not feel pressured. It's true, a PA would have changed the process. And actually going into the studio was one of those moments where I realized I had to come in with something. I couldn't just not know how the song went at a certain point. I really needed to have ideas, and so the process of having to record forced me into making sure I really had the ideas that I wanted. The whole time that we would play live I could do anything I wanted, but when you go into the studio you can't really play fast and loose like that. And plus, in the studio Ian or Don, or Natalie, Kate, or Nicky, would say, "What if we did this instead?" or, "Try this." That was part of the process. And that is very useful to me and I'm into that, honestly.

Williams: What's it like to revisit the music again many years later?

Pickering: I have to say, I listened to a song today and I was like, *This song is exactly what it is supposed to be and it's really tight and it's really powerful and it hits all the marks for me.* In past times, I could never listen to myself. It's a very, very different experience. But listening now, I'm less exacting about myself and learning, critiquing myself. I can now hear the whole song and before I heard parts.

Avery: I'll say one thing really quickly. Nicky is just an amazing drummer. Like thinking about the rhythm section. And Kate too.

Nicky Thomas: It's funny because I feel like the further away we've gotten from it, the better it sounds to me. And maybe it's because I feel like I can have distance from it. Whoever that person was is so different from who I am now that it just sounds different to me, and it still sounds pretty amazing. But I think definitely my ears are way more mature now when I listen to things. I think I would listen to things before and like maybe I would hear the drums, maybe I would listen to the singer, but now I can really parse things out and understand textures of music and production a little bit more. So yeah, it's just really fulfilling to listen back to it now.

One Last Wish - Snakes

One Last Wish, twelve-song tape session, 1986. TOP LEFT: (left to right) Brendan Canty, Eddie Janney, Don Zientara, Guy Picciotto, and Ian MacKaye. TOP RIGHT: Eddie Janney (left) and Don Zientara. MIDDLE LEFT: (left to right) Eddie Janney, Brendan Canty, and Michael Hampton. MIDDLE RIGHT: Don Zientara (blurred) and Ian MacKaye. BOTTOM LEFT: Ian MacKaye (left) and Guy Picciotto. BOTTOM CENTER: Brendan Canty. Photos by Jeff Nelson. BOTTOM RIGHT: Snakes, *I Won't Love You* session, 1985. (Clockwise from left) Ian MacKaye, Simon Jacobsen, Michael Hampton, Guy Picciotto, and Don. Photos courtesy of Don Zientara.

Lawrence McDonald

Bells Of..

We were all sponsored vert skateboarders but we never identified as a "sk8" band—it was a moot point. We skated during the day and at night we played music. When the time came to finally start recording Bells Of's first tunes, I wanted it to be unique.

Inner Ear (Don's first location) was a special space and sounded great. Although the room was quite small it had a unique warmth that made one feel at home and was a conduit for producing great local music.

I tried my best to duplicate that same feel when I acquired the original Teac 80-8 that Don used to record so many great hardcore classics. Owning that same reel-to-reel, along with all the musical history spit onto its analog heads, made me feel that I had a key piece of the puzzle. Upon designing my own home studio (potentially trying to create the same atmosphere Don had on South Ivy), I had only moderate success—the setup and room sound he had in his cozy basement always outshined anything I could ever put together.

When bands recorded at Inner Ear, Don was always very careful to try and preserve the artists' vision without intervening or tainting the concept of their songs. However, he was very "hands on" at times and would subtly suggest alternatives—things a recording artist may not have been aware of.

In writing this, I think back to the first Bells Of.. record, *00/85*, conceived at Inner Ear. As a seventeen-year-old patron of Don's, I would reach an impasse with a particular song and he was always available to consult with his thoughtful and insightful ideas to help reignite any creative fire that may have temporarily smoldered.

Pete Chramiec

Verbal Assault - Rain Like the Sound of Trains

Our first Inner Ear trip was a little atypical for the time as we were really young (just turned seventeen), from way out of town (Newport, RI), and Ian didn't really record bands that weren't from DC at the time. It was a little like we had won some kind of national lottery.

Brendan, Guy, and Mike Fellows stopped by the Dischord House that evening and instead of being the thespian poets I had imagined, they passed around a little bottle of peppermint oil, daring each other to take more drops until all their mouths were numb and they couldn't control their lips or words or drool.

It was then that I determined that I should move there.

The Straight Line

50¢

WINTER 1985 ISSUE # 2

SECTION 25

1/2 JAPS

DON ZIENTARA AND IAN MACKAYE

IN THE STUDIO - -

The Straight Line fanzine, 1985, by Mark Robinson, Wakefield High School in Arlington, Virginia.

IN THE STUDIO WITH DON ZIENTARA & IAN MAC KAYE

Don Zientara and Ian MacKaye were interviewed at Zientara's Inner Ear recording studio by Tim. When we arrived, a hardcore group called Seven Seconds was being recorded. A great deal of attention was being paid to the details. The recording room is an old boiler room packed full with equipment. Also present were Richard, Lily, and Wolfgang. October 21, 1984.

Tim: How did you get this equipment, and how long did it take? Ten years?
Don: No, about 4 or 5.
Tim: What did you start with?
Don: I used to only have astereo recorder.
Tim: Do you remember what your first recording was?
Don: Geez, the Look, the Slickee Boys, some of my own stuff; it's hard to recall.
Tim: What do you play?
Don: Guitar, but very rarely anymore.
Tim: Were you in a group?
Don: Yeah, Ravenstone, a folk-rock band during the mid-seventies.
Tim: Do you consider recording a hobby, an obsession, or work?
Don: All of them. It's a hobby and it sort of regenerates itself because it supports the fact that more stuff builds on the equipment.
Tim: Do you record every weekend?
Daon: More like everyday.
Ian: Guess what his other job is.
Tim: You record chamber music?
Don: Well, not anymore. I work at Cutting Studios, a radio commercial studio.
Tim: You keep busy then?
Don: Yeah, but it's a lot of fun. You know, this is where the music is. In the commercial studio you use what's available on the market, a lot of professional stuff, but here, everything is pretty much traditional.
Tim: What records do you buy?
Don: I buy very few records—play very few. Sometimes I'll play an old tape that I've done. I listen to the radio, though. You have to listen to outside work to get an idea of what is being done. You have to have something to compare your own work to.
Richard: What's your favorite record that you have recorded? Minor Threat?
Don: I really don't know. There's a lot of music that's very different. Basically, the type of music I like working with is original, and rock-n-roll.
Tim: What are a few groups you've done recently?
Don: Just the other night the Concentric, a very electic group. Very weird music, weird beats. Also, the Velvet Monkeys. That's still being mixed.
Tim: Once you get done recording, is it a big hassle getting something pressed?
Don: I don't know.
Ian: He does the recording.
Tim: (to Ian) Is it a pain dealing with the pressing companies?
Ian: It depends on who it is and their mood.
Tim: What's the process?
Ian: It's all a big orchestration. That's what the record companies are all about, just orchestrating all the bullshit.
Tim: How is your studio different from other area studios?
Don: I put my emphasis on different things. I hate to bring up specifics because it'll just distort the point, but the emphasis si on different parts of things.
Ian: I don't think there's anything like it.
Tim: (to Ian) What are you doing now?
Ian: I haven't got a band together yet, working on it. Life's a bitch in the big time.
Wolfgang: What's the truth about Dischord (Records)?
Ian: Oh, we're definitely almost dead. It's not any fun to do be in something that I consider shouldn't be like a business, and then to have it be like a job or business. I didn't want to be a company. I want to be spontaneous and creative, not motivated by money. It's very hard to do though.

Don then invited us to see the other rooms, the studios. The main studio is merely an ordinary den. But aside from a rug and furniture, there are various sound baffles and an array of microphones. The separate vocalist's studio is a concrete-walled laundry room.

the end

SUN CITY GIRLS <u>Sun City Girls</u> (Placebo)

<u>Sun City Girls</u> is truly a raucous sound that just shouldn't be missed. If you saw them live with Jodie Foster's Army in July, you were entranced. Although <u>Sun City Girls</u> does not fully capture their live essence, it does sound like there were no retakes.

Many of their songs have a very raw or somewhat unpolished sound; but it's a nice switch to hear from the mechanically polished sound of pop. Some of their songs are forgettable, but many stay with you.

"Uncle Jim" is a humorous monologue backed by wretched jazz in which "Jim" talds about his ... life. In his own words, he "spews a li... on us. The pure insanity of "... Ending Magic Trick" is ... Tent" follows. ... of surf ...

Scott McCloud

Soulside - Girls Against Boys

The experience of recording in "studios" has changed so much since the mid-1980s that it's hard to know where to begin, and where to put Don Zientara in this spectrum. Obviously Don was the first of a kind. There is a lot of mystification about the "recording process" dating back into "rock history," most of which is greatly exaggerated. A recording studio is typically a place that has a "good-sounding room" which usually means a big room, and usually that means for drums more than anything else. Big rooms. Big drum sound. And lots of flashy "gear," meaning little things that light up even when no one knows what they mean (and it's usually not much).

Don Zientara had none of these things in the '80s. His studio was simply a basement room underneath his very ordinary suburban Arlington home. There was no fanfare. No big room. Dinner was usually served to the band together with his family (maybe a bowl of spaghetti), and sessions were strictly on the clock of a suburban neighborhood. No real noise after let's say eight p.m. And sessions that I participated in would rarely have run later than that. This was not an all-nighter type of studio. Don Z., himself, would have surprised young punks trying to record there. He was not punk at all in terms of fashion, but instead, a very tall, physically super-fit triathlete, with a smiling face welcoming you.

One of the great things about Don was, due to the temperatures in virtually any season, the studio would get hot. He always wore these incredibly high-cut tiny sports shorts. His legs seemed longer than an average human body. He and his seemingly incredibly long legs could barely fit his figure down the stairs. But once down there, in his perch in front of the board, he was absolutely at home and seemingly always in an incredible mood of openness, kindness, indeed, happiness. I always wondered how he could be so happy, in his basement, recording this stuff. Which at the time seemed just a bunch of kids.

Soulside, *Trigger* session, 1987: (left to right) Johnny Temple, Bobby Sullivan (hidden in back), Ian MacKaye, and Scott McCloud. Photo by Alexis Fleisig.

But he didn't mind at all. I guess, after all, he was at home, literally, so there was really no pressure for him.

Don was incredibly sweet to work with on the few occasions I had the chance. One thing he told me was a comment on one of the songs for *Trigger* during the Soulside recording. I was doing a very repetitive guitar riff and he very discreetly took me aside for a comment and said, "It's great, I get that you like repetition, but maybe you should also try finishing the riff slightly differently sometimes. Maybe on the third pass out of four?"

Fugazi, *Red Medicine* session, 1995. Ian MacKaye in the corner chair. Photo by Jem Cohen.

This left a lasting impression. Of course it's Music Theory 101 in retrospect, which I didn't know at all then, at nineteen or whatever, but he didn't really need to take the time to tell a kid like me this little nugget of wisdom. He just wanted to make a suggestion.

It wasn't so much what he told me, but the way he told me. Without any indication of being "better than" me, more like an honest observation. Meant in the humblest of senses. Not meant to interfere. Just a suggestion. To push myself just a little harder in the vision. And I've never forgotten it.

Ian MacKaye

Teen Idles - Minor Threat - Embrace - Fugazi - The Evens - Coriky

In late 1981, Minor Threat started working on the *In My Eyes* 7". We decided to include our cover version of the Monkees's song "Steppin' Stone," but realized that the only version we had was a rough mix on cassette. The master was on a four-track tape that we had recorded earlier in the year at Inner Ear Studio as part of the band's first session. We needed a proper stereo master of the song to send to the pressing plant, so I called Don and asked him if he would throw together a mix for us, figuring that our sound was straightforward enough for him to do it without us being present. At that time, I had a fairly fundamentalist view of how punk music should sound, meaning stripped down with no studio trickery. Vérité.

Don was happy to help out and called me a couple days later to let me know I could pick up the finished tape. I went to his house and down into the basement studio to hear the results. The first thing that came out of the speakers was me goofing around with the piano and talking, but the sound was extremely thin and bright like it was coming over a transistor radio. Then the song began in the same tiny frequency. At first I couldn't figure out what was happening and thought that something must be wrong with his speakers, but then with each measure the individual instruments one by one started to fill with proper tone until the body of the song kicked in with full force.

I was furious.

Did Don think our music was some sort of joke? I had specifically asked him to just do a straight mix, similar to the rest of our songs, and he had toyed with the sounds and come up with something that at first sounded extremely weird and, furthermore, something that we would never be able to reproduce onstage. This didn't sit well with my above-stated sonic fundamentalism.

This happened almost half a century ago, so I can't recall the exact exchange, but my recollection is that I yelled at Don for taking liberties with our music and wondered what the hell he was thinking. He responded with something to the effect that it was just an idea that had occurred to him while getting the sounds together, so he did it.

It was the fact that it was such an open-and-shut case for him that I think drove me so nuts. He felt it, he heard it, he did it. I was getting a proper schooling about the creative possibilities of sound and it knocked me out of my safe and rudimentary understanding of music art.

In any event, Don wasn't upset by my upset, instead I think he just played the song again and my ears and brain began to acclimate to what had initially struck me as an insane and insulting treatment. His mix of "Steppin' Stone" started to sound cool, really cool.

Fugazi, *Red Medicine* session, 1995. Joe Lally in the corner chair. Photo by Jem Cohen.

In fact, I loved it.

I often refer to Don as a "superhero" and I mean it. He may not have flown in to save the world, but he definitely created one. It's a world that I've been a part of and one that has been a part of me for decades.

Joe Lally

Fugazi - Messthetics - Coriky

I had been in a couple of studios before, so I had some idea what to expect when Fugazi went to Inner Ear to record our first demo. Even so, I was surprised that he did nothing to make the basement studio-like. To record there was very much being welcomed into his home. When he moved into a larger space he carried a lot of that atmosphere of home by surrounding the place with art of a very childlike nature. All of the sessions at home and then in the bigger space in Shirlington all sort of blend into one experience for me, so I find it difficult to comment on a particular session. A band isolates itself from the rest of the world and imagines its own landscape in music to tell a story. Walking outside you can be surprised it's still daylight or by something else that suggests you've lost track of time.

The main thing I remember about recording there is that Don is present, but not in the way. He gives his opinion, but you know the band has to decide what's what.

Sometime around 2006, I was amazed to hear Don was playing solo shows. After all those years he was recording other bands, I had never seen him play. The Desperados were pictured on the wall of the studio, but I never saw a show. I don't know what I expected, but the first time I saw him play, I was intrigued. The contrast of his look and the sound of the music he was making didn't quite fit. Don's a tall guy with a pleasant demeanor, but now he seemed imposing and a bit . . . off. Had he served in Vietnam? Did he take too many hallucinogens at some point in the past? His hair is close cut and neat and he only wears shorts and flip-flops no matter what the weather is like. Deranged surfer? His voice could bellow in such a way that it overwhelmed the little sound system in the room. His acoustic guitar had some kind of chorus from a little mixer he ran it through, which put the songs on edge. It all sounded dark. I was a little scared, and I liked it.

He came out to see my first solo show in a record store and sometime after that I came up with the idea of booking us a little tour. Someone from Bowling Green, KY, contacted me so I figured the tour would peak there, and we'd turn back toward home. I guess there were about seven or eight shows in coffee shops and small bars. Don drove us in his Toyota sedan. We put my bass, small amp, and 1x12 cabinet in the backseat along with his acoustic guitar and small mixer. I don't think the radio worked in the car. If it did, we never turned it on. We would talk some and then just listen to the wind and the cars. We could go for miles and not say a word. It always felt comfortable and relaxing. He would give me pointers about playing, and I needed them. I was forcing myself to do something that I didn't understand so I could learn how to do it properly. We'd stay with someone who put us up and I would always wake up about an hour before Don because I would start thinking about everything going on that day. He slept like a baby. His conscience seemed clear. He made great food at a group house we stayed at once. Everyone we met liked him.

Two days before Inner Ear closes its doors, I'm putting down backing vocals on some Coriky songs. We listen to the lead vocal and I try something to complement it. Don rewinds the tape so I can take another shot at it. It's easy and we finish

Fugazi

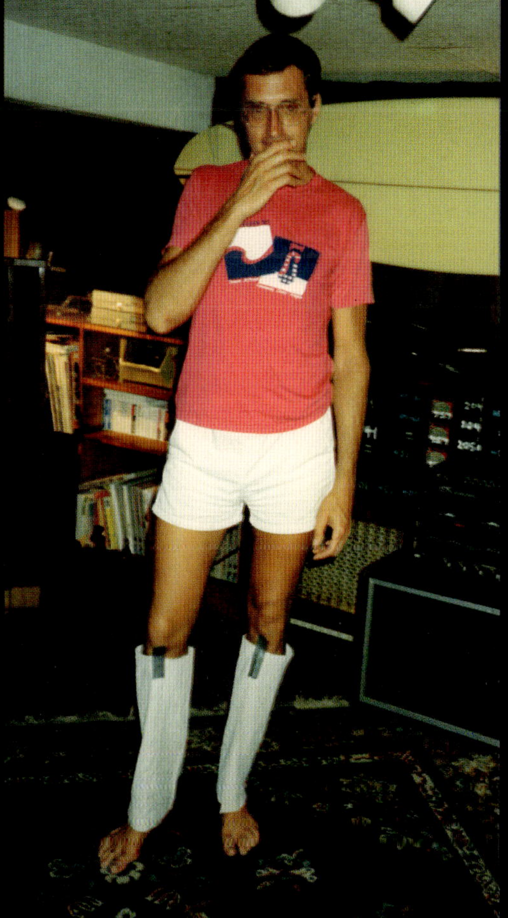

Fugazi, *Seven Songs* session, 1989. TOP LEFT: (left to right) Ted Niceley, Ian MacKaye, and Brendan Canty. TOP CENTER: (left to right) Ted Niceley, Ian MacKaye, and Brendan Canty. Photos courtesy of Fugazi.

Three Songs session, 1989. TOP RIGHT: Brendan Canty. MIDDLE LEFT: Ian MacKaye (left) and Ted Niceley. MIDDLE RIGHT: Don Zientara. BOTTOM: Fugazi's dryer. Photos courtesy of Fugazi.

Fugazi, *Red Medicine* session, 1995. Brendan Canty in the corner chair. Photo by Jem Cohen.

quickly. I look forward to doing this again with Don and this band or any band, studio or no studio.

Brendan Canty

Rites of Spring - Fugazi - Messthetics

Trying to surmise the depth of meaning that one person whom you've known for forty years has on your own life is like trying to describe your own mother to someone. One is rarely able to spend more than a sentence or two on the subject before giving over to the futility of it, resorting to a couple grunting compliments before trailing off. "She was brilliant. So funny . . . lovely . . ."

Don Zientara, like my mother, was foundationally influential to me. Not as much for what he was, but for what he *wasn't*. He wasn't an asshole. He wasn't judgmental. He didn't talk down to the fifteen-year-old me recording drums in his basement for the first time in 1981. He may have noticed I didn't use my kick drum much, as I hadn't been playing for more than a couple weeks, but he never mentioned it. He would crack a joke and place his mic. His humor bent toward surrealism, though that may have been a congenital dad gene he couldn't shake. There were always kids around. Kids toys all over the benches in the basement.

I recorded every year of the '80s there. I only remember sporadic bits of it, and yet I remember every inch of the space and many of the equalizers on the wall. He encouraged us to get in there and fiddle around with the knobs. He wasn't precious. It was always fun. If a session wasn't fun, it wasn't his fault, and usually those are the bands that broke up soon after anyway. It's a real litmus test for a band and an engineer—whether or not you can keep your humor level up and balance everyone's emotions in what can be a high-pressure environment. He was without a doubt unflappable, impossible to anger, and downright jolly 99 percent of the time.

Deadline, Insurrection, Rites of Spring, One Last Wish, Fugazi. That's the '80s mostly for me, and all but the *Margin Walker* EP was recorded at Don's. By the end of the '80s Don moved and we continued to record all through the '90s at the bigger space. It always felt like home and he always welcomed our fingers on the faders and EQs. I learned so much from all of it. Mostly I learned that the atmosphere in a room translates onto tape. That the more comfortable and supported you feel, the more chances you take. That hearing each other in the room is super important. I carry with me all these lessons—I use them in the studio and I use them with my kids. Don's congenital dad gene has been passed down to us all. Don Zientara? Brilliant, so funny . . . lovely.

Guy Picciotto

Insurrection - Rites of Spring - Fugazi

The first time I went to Inner Ear Studio was in 1982 as a sixteen-year-old hanger-on at a recording session with the band Deadline. At one point I got invited to do some backup vocals, shouting, "Authority figures! False heroes!" at the top of my lungs. It was the first time I had ever been recorded on tape that wasn't housed in a janky Maxell cassette inside a boom box, and in that moment I felt an excitement beyond all proportion to my minor contribution. Being in that tight basement amid the action of making a record felt like the most significant place on the face of the earth, and all I wanted was to do it again and again.

The last time I went to Inner Ear Studio was in November of 2019 to mix the Casual Dots's *Sanguine Truth* album. The studio was no longer housed in Don's basement but the fundamental vibe of the place was intact, as was Don's positive, forward-thinking energy. In the thirty-seven years between Deadline and the Dots, my life has been fully centered around music, and the great majority of recordings I've been involved with have been with Don at the board—from my first band Insurrection to Rites of Spring to One Last Wish to Fugazi and beyond. With all that shared history, to try and nutshell the impact Don and

Fugazi, *Red Medicine* session, 1995. Guy Picciotto in th corner chair. Photo by Jem Cohen.

Inner Ear has had on my life is ultimately paralyzing—it is just too total. Instead, here is one random memory that comes to mind that sort of encapsulates what I love about the man and the space he created:

In 1985 while working on the Rites of Spring album with Don, we had just one night to mix the whole record. It was getting pretty late when we came to the final song, "End on End," and we were all feeling a bit dizzy and burnt. Forty seconds into working on the song, we realized that we had forgotten to track Mike Fellows's backing vocal—a shouted "Go!" that came in right before the second verse starts. It was a small thing but it was something he always did live and we were attached to it—the song just felt weird to us without it. Asked if it was really necessary, we were adamant—it had to be on there. To give some context, we had spent the whole session doing stuff like tracking in the pitch dark with just a strobe light going, tackling each other during takes, using two distortion boxes in sequence on Eddie's guitar, etc. To his great credit, Don objected to none of it, but facing this last-minute perverse insistence on rectifying the missing "Go!" he may have worried the night was going to unspool into more endless nonsense. He also probably wasn't excited at the prospect of having to switch his board over from "mixing mode" to "tracking mode" for such a small vocal. Instead, he suggested Mike just shout "Go!" into the tiny talkback microphone located on the corner of the mixing console (a *talkback* is the microphone engineers use to communicate with musicians over their headphones or to slate songs onto tape in the manner of "'Mustang Sally'—take one!").

The talkback vocal overdub idea seemed like a reasonable move until we realized that recording via the console in that manner goes over all eight tracks of the tape, thereby erasing whatever was previously on those eight tracks—i.e., the song itself. In the split second that it took for Mike to shout "Go!" into the mixing desk, all the music disappeared into a black hole before coming roaring back in as Don released the talkback button. Stunned, we were all not exactly sure what had just happened—was it okay? Was this normal operating procedure? Was it technically allowed? Ultimately, it didn't matter what the answer to those questions was because there was no way to reverse it—it was a done deal, so we just moved on and finished the song. I will say, over the years no one outside of the band ever seems to have noticed it—amidst all the chaos going on in that song, that "Go!" just gets in line behind all those other bits of madness, but it's definitely there: a voice that seems to beam in out of nowhere, for a millisecond obliterating all else.

I'm sure some perfectionists would see this as an engineering faux pas of epic proportions, but the truth is, those types of anomalies are often exactly the kinds of details that you treasure in a recording. In the Beatles's song "If I Fell," there is a cracked note in one of the otherwise immaculate backing vocals that I hear every time—should they have corrected it somehow? Probably, but they were working against the clock and they let it slide and now it's a detail that I look forward to every time I play the song. The lesson I learned from this was: some things matter in recording, some things don't, and it's not always obvious which is which.

That lesson took awhile to sink in. Six years later, Fugazi was recording the album *Steady Diet of Nothing*. I had amassed a bunch more experience making records in the years in between, but I was still at the perfectly terrible conjunction of knowing enough about recording to be obsessively suspicious about the process but still not really savvy enough to understand what was actually significant. As a result, I spent an inordinate amount of time in a state of paranoia about the processing gear involved—desperately concerned that somehow the "integrity" of our music was being compromised by the blinking lights and dials that surrounded me and that I didn't fully understand. Don's reaction was always to try to point me back to the music itself and my proper role as someone who should be thinking about that music instead. He was basically saying, "Stop staring at the Avalon AD2044 opto-compressor like it is a serial abuser and just fucking relax and use your ears to listen." The point is not that you can't make bad aesthetic decisions with gear but rather that the mindset you cultivate in the studio is directly linked to what comes out of the studio. You can absolutely poison your ability to do the thing you are trying to do if you let your creativity get sidetracked into pointless cul-de-sacs, most of which have to do with gear, proper procedure, or "technique." The old saw that a literal ape at the controls can't ruin a great song and the greatest engineer in the world can't save a bad one is a simple truth. That doesn't mean you shouldn't try to perfect the craft of recording—it just means, don't get confused about what that craft ultimately is.

That is Don's greatest trait as an engineer and producer—his priorities lie with the act of creating things, not enforcing a signature sound or a contemporary approach, meter-hawking, or gear-fetishization. The thing I've heard him say the most over the years is, "Let's try it!" which is always the right answer to almost everything, in the studio or elsewhere. This is not to say that Don doesn't have amazing technical chops. Listen to what he did with a four-track on Minor Threat's "Steppin' Stone," which moves through all the different ports of call of fidelity before exploding into its final rich power—to me it's hardcore's "Day in the Life." That song proved to me that Don is fundamentally an experimental artist. When Fugazi came back from tour talking up how much we loved wood floor stages for their resonance on the drums, he promptly built a raised wooden floor in his tracking room that very morning, right before we started tracking. He and Steve Gamboa just dove in with power saws and drills and some plywood and made us a stage. There was no guarantee it would work, but the drums sounded great and the raised floor stayed there for the rest of the life of the studio as the physical embodiment of Don's willingness to go for it in the name of experimentation.

People always comment on the atmosphere of Inner Ear with all its toys, puzzles, stuffed animals, and bursts of color on the walls, but all that stuff is ultimately simply functional because Don knows the playful mind is the creative mind, and Don is nothing if not playful: he's the adult in the room who was never the adult in the room because no one needs an adult in the room.

Alex Daniels

Carpe Diem - Swiz

I recorded lots of music with the band Swiz at Inner Ear at its warehouse location, but my first experience there (my first experience at any professional studio) was when it was in Don's Arlington basement. The session was with Carpe Diem, a band I played drums in during my junior year of high school. I remember getting lost a number of times driving over there for the first time (this is a common occurrence for Maryland drivers in Virginia who are not accustomed to the assortment of Glebe Roads that seem to sprout out from all directions across the Potomac), and my directions kept taking me by a suburban rambler with the address I was given.

I thought—*This is it?*—fully expecting that the studio would be in some office or warehouse location to house the stacks and stacks of gadgetry I imagined it had. When I went around back, and down the stairs into the studio for the first time, I saw that Don sure did have a lot of gadgets, but they were economically stowed in a cozy den of an engineer's booth, with a recording room right next door.

What I quickly learned at Don's was that he had built it all himself. That he wanted to record music, and he had the expertise to take all of this equipment, an ordinary basement, and refashion it into a place where people could come and be creative. That level of craftiness and ability—and vision, really—was amazing to me.

The recording session was fun. Previously I had recorded songs on portable four-track recorders and the experience was pretty trying. Don set everything up, and was extremely patient with us as he listened to a bunch of high schoolers describe the masterpiece they wanted to create. He took us really seriously. The whole time it felt like we were equals, and there wasn't a hint of condescension or the slightest raised eyebrow on his part as we talked through what would strengthen each track.

This was important for me to see, because Derek Denckla, who was pretty much the leader of the band, was extremely talented and had a lot to say in his music. And sitting in the studio for the first time listening on playback, as my fidgety teenage hands played with one of the handheld distractor toys Don had strategically placed around the control booth (I think so we wouldn't start spinning knobs and sliding volume slides), I finally pieced together the bass lines Chad Houseknecht wove into each song, and could hear, without it being muddled in the mix, the lyrical solo lines that Ravi Ricker was playing on the guitar. Through recording at Don's, I could, for the first time, hear the songs we had been practicing in the basement for months.

Did we create a masterpiece? I don't think so. But in taking us seriously, Don helped our musical ideas develop more completely. It's still fun to listen to the tape we made.

Craig Wedren

Shudder to Think

Shudder to Think recorded at Inner Ear, but the sheer velocity of young life and ambition, combined with creative possession and the strange game of time and memory, have left me with a clear feeling rather than an accurate memory.

And the feeling, I think, may have more to do with Don Z. himself than Inner Ear, although the studio seemed to me to be an extension and expression of Don's energy and philosophy: lean, open-minded/hearted, outside of time and trends, practical, and above all creative and encouraging in an unfussy way.

I suspect we took some of these rare qualities for granted at the time. But I'm struck now at how deeply Don's—and by extension Inner Ear's—gestalt has become part of my own.

I owe an even greater debt of gratitude, practically and philosophically, to Dischord Records and Ian MacKaye, for whom Inner Ear was also an obvious and natural extension, and I wonder to what extent Ian's and Dischord's ethos was similarly shaped by Don's and Inner Ear's overt and covert hand. Suffice to say, they are of a piece in my heart and mind, Inner Ear and Dischord, both completely sensible and utterly idiosyncratic all at once, like so many of my favorite inspiring beings and things.

I had the pleasure of touring briefly with Don in the early 2000s—it was him, me, and Joe Lally doing solo living room shows—and that's when it really struck me what a treasure Don and his creations really are, whether musical, technical, or conversational. Watching him live, and chatting between shows, really connected some pieces for me, helped me understand why Inner Ear was such a unique magnet for magic.

I've spent lots of time listening to the records and imagining the sessions—Rites of Spring in particular comes to mind—and the frame, the home, the ambiance and hearth, are always Inner Ear, obviously. Anywhere else, it just doesn't work. No clubhouse romance.

Put it in another studio—Electric Lady, for instance—and the energy changes so radically it's almost comedic, ridiculous. Something vital would be lost. It's so hard to relax and play at most recording studios—you have to kind of trick your mind into it. I don't remember that being a thought at Inner Ear; it was just like, *Here's a sandbox, let's throw dirt.* At least that's how I like to think of it, and certainly how I imagine it when I dream of all those records.

I hope that, as studios and real estate change, and change hands, that the spark of Inner Ear—that easy framework within which so much fearsome beauty and risk-taking was splattered onto tape—is merely transferred to those of us who got to play there. Maybe *we* were the magnetic tape.

I know that my studio, the way I like to use it, resembles more an experimental family kitchen than a Hit Factory. I suspect Inner Ear is at least partly to blame.

Jason Farrell

Swiz - Bluetip - Sweetbelly Freakdown - Retisonic

My band Swiz was among the first . . . maybe the first . . . to record in Inner Ear's second location. The studio wasn't 100 percent done, but even in its early stages the space sounded fucking great: a legit studio with all the trappings. It was a huge step up from out of the basement—the original space where Swiz had recorded everything else. Yet somehow this new space still managed to keep the innovative and welcoming spirit of its predecessor. This was clearly due to the energy of Don. His openness, patience, and creativity have always been a godsend to musicians struggling to articulate and capture their sound.

Years later I was in the new space with Ian and Don recording vocals for another band, Bluetip. Ninety percent of that was relatively easy—I just had to yell—but this one song needed something intimate. I was so reliant on hiding behind volume and force that I felt exposed without them. Cranking the playback volume in my headphones did little to fix this feeling. Don calmly began a series of adjustments to the space: dimming the lights, moving baffles, laying me on my back. He then handed me a second set of headphones, one I was meant to sing into, held like a teacup. The spooky natural compression that played back in my ears allowed me to sing barely above a whisper.

Don's calming enthusiasm could fill any studio, but I really loved recording with him in that original basement. The history was heavy down there, knowing the stuffed animals around the rumpus room had witnessed with their plastic eyes my favorite records getting made, movements being born. The soft audience helped mitigate intimidation, sitting dumb with their felt tongues stuck out. But seeing the names of my favorite bands on row after row of white boxes, all scrawled in Don's loopy handwriting, was a stark reminder that this cozy, humble space had explosive possibilities.

Marc Lambiotte

Holy Rollers

From the moment we knew we were recording in Inner Ear's "big room," the excitement and anticipation was immense. We had passed on a similar opportunity to record our first record there, and considered ourselves very fortunate to have a second shot at making a record at this iconic studio. In fact, we were fortunate enough to record *two* records there.

The studio itself was well equipped with a mixture of state-of-the-art and vintage equipment, all at our disposal. The low-lit control room was so comfortable. It felt like we were hanging out in our living room. Don's style was relaxed and accommodating. We would describe a sound or idea and he would think about it a minute and then help us set something up that fit the bill perfectly. He worked with our engineer in full partnership and there was never any conflict or negativity.

Guest vocalists? No problem. Mic'd speaker under a snare drum to get a fuzzy, tinny vocal track? No problem. Screaming distorted guitar track via Don's Fender Super Champ? Sure thing! Clapping audience sound effects? Done! The entire experience was jovial, collaborative, and supportive of achieving our vision.

When it came time for final mixing, Don was a trusted partner and worked with producers and the band to arrive at the final mixes. The use of his vintage tube amplifiers added a warmth and presence that we loved and carried through to the masters. Don honed in on the sound we were after and made it happen! It was so much fun and amazing to watch the master at work. I'll always remember fondly those many days, and nights, spent in the brick building off Four Mile Run in Arlington, Virginia. Cheers to you, Don, and thank you!

Mitchell Feldstein

Lungfish

In a recent text with Antonia, I said I was having difficulty thinking of something to write about my experience(s) recording with Don at Inner Ear, as working with him just seemed so effortless. Then it hit me like a bolt of lightning.

Don's true gift was making things work smoothly and effortlessly. He laid the groundwork, got the instruments mic'd properly, the levels set, had the lighting just right, knew when to interject, when to lay back, and had just the right toys to keep the musicians occupied when they weren't busy playing, listening, bitching, arguing, and also, in our case, chain-smoking.

I was lucky enough to spend a lot of time on a number of occasions with Don at Inner Ear. He put up with us from near our beginning to what I guess is considered our extended hiatus. For that I am grateful, and whatever the next chapter brings, I know Don will handle it with grace and aplomb.

Thanks, Don.

Sean Meadows

Lungfish - June of 44

Lungfish had already made three great sounding records with Don by the time I first walked into Inner Ear Studio. Because Don struck me as someone who could have done anything he wanted to with his talents, and that his passion was for recording music, I felt a certain pressure to deliver the most focused results. However, there never seemed to be any pressure anywhere near Don. His affable, gentle, silky-smooth demeanor and disposition didn't accommodate any space for pressure, and with his ever-present abilities and lightness of being, the atmosphere, to my very young and impressionable faculties, seemed to be charged with possibilities, nurtured by this sense of trust and respect that Don, in his lumbering frame, surfer khakis, and T-shirt, radiated in his studio.

Working with Don and Lungfish taught me that one way to achieve a sense of balance while working on music that is extremely important to you is to NOT take yourself too seriously, to engage in communication with your collaborators with banter if that is your inclination, but in a way that's light and supportive.

They didn't talk about any of this, they were just working, and I was learning by observation. I find the experiences making these records with Don incomparable to any other musical experience I've ever had, in the sense that spending valuable hours with Don, I had thi s feeling that he was capable of making and/or teaching complicated things in a simple manner. Now, this may be a gift he has, but my sense is it's also one he's nurtured and developed.

The records are cool, I'm very proud of them, but the time I spent in the presence of Don, working with him and Mitchell, Daniel, Asa, and Ian too . . . that's what I value most. I'm grateful to have had that experience, working together, making music.

Lungfish outside Inner Ear, *Love Is Love* session, 2003. (Left to right) Mitchell Feldstein, Sean Meadows, Daniel Higgs, and Asa Osborne. Photo by Antonia Tricarico.

Lungfish, *Necrophones* session, 2000. TOP: Nathan Bell (left) and Joe Lally. MIDDLE: Ian MacKaye (left) and Asa Osborne. BOTTOM: (left to right) Daniel Higgs, Mitchell Feldstein, and Don Zientara.

velocity

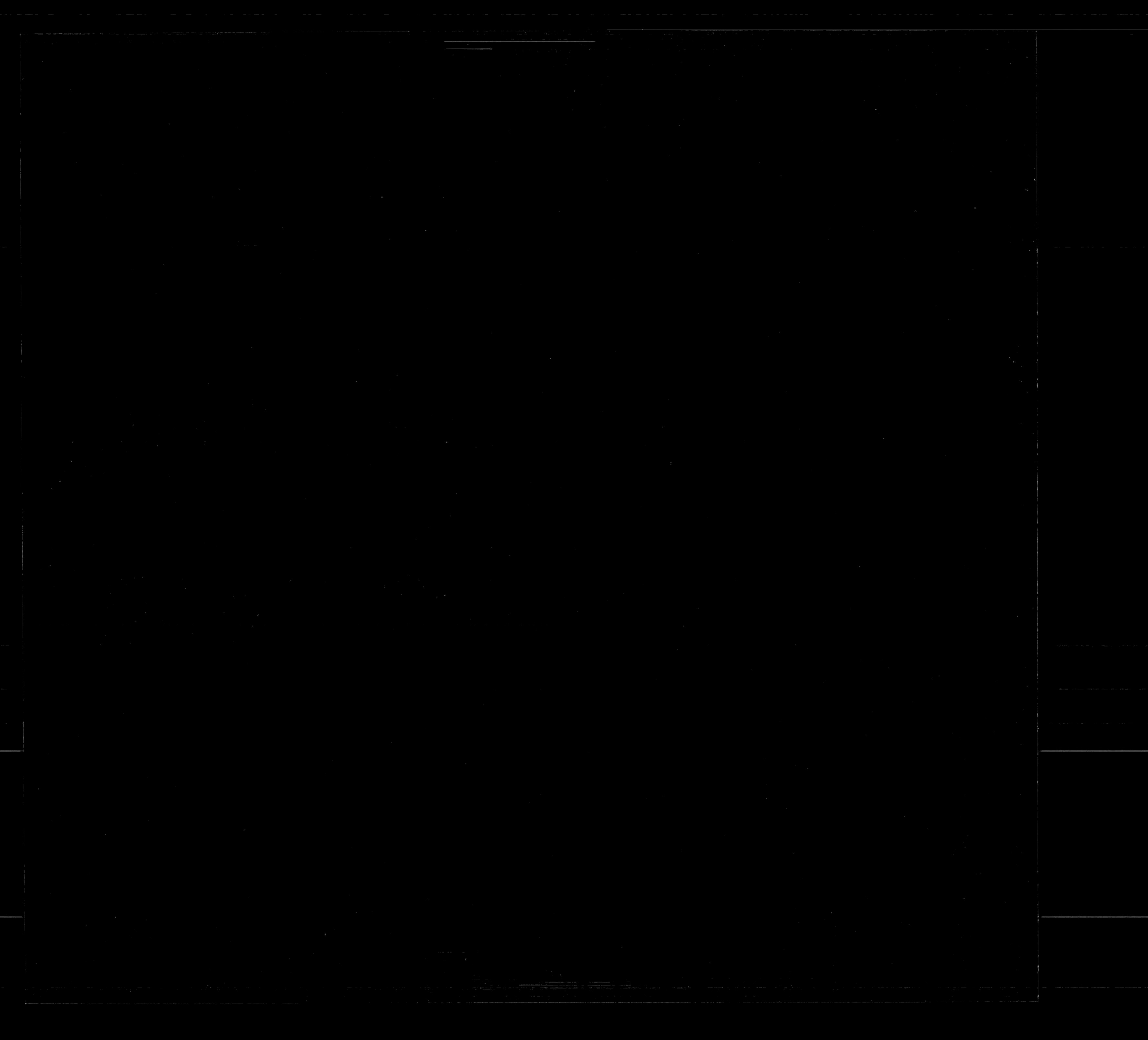

Part II

Inner Ear
(1990-2021)

Inner Ear logo made by Jeff Nelson in 1990. Photo by Antonia Tricarico.

HIS PAGE

nner Ear new location under renovation, 1990. TOP LEFT: Jeff Nelson (far back) and Ian MacKaye. TOP RIGHT: (left to right) Don, Jeff Nelson, and Jim Freeman. MIDDLE LEFT: Jeff Nelson taking photographs. MIDDLE RIGHT: Building materials for the new space. BOTTOM: Ian MacKaye (left) and Jeff Nelson.

PPOSITE PAGE

nner Ear new location under renovation, 1990. TOP LEFT: (left to right) im Freeman, Don Zientara, Jeff Nelson, Ian MacKaye, and Amanda MacKaye. Photo courtesy of Don Zientara. TOP RIGHT: Ian MacKaye. Photo courtesy of Don Zientara. MIDDLE LEFT: Jim Freeman. Photo courtesy of Don Zientara. MIDDLE RIGHT: Jim Freeman. Photo by Jeff Nelson. BOTTOM LEFT: Don Zientara (left) and Jim Freeman. Photo by Jeff Nelson. BOTTOM RIGHT: (left to right) Ian MacKaye, Amanda MacKaye, and Jim Freeman. Photo by Jeff Nelson.

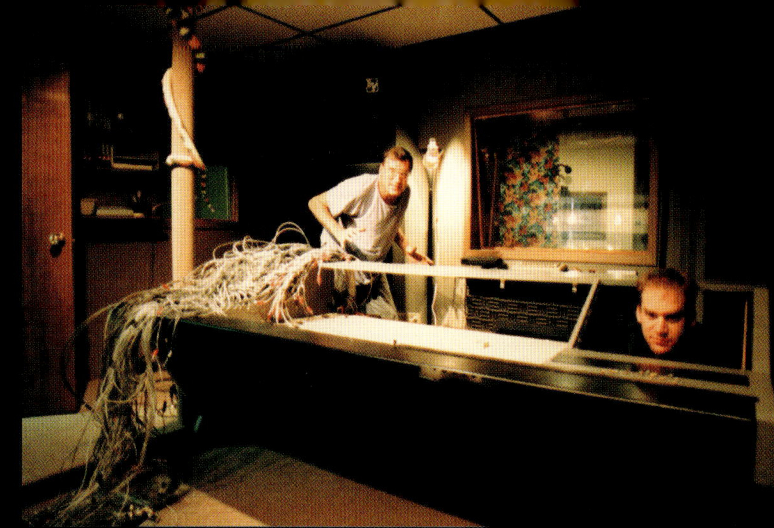

nner Ear new location, 1992. TOP LEFT: building the new mixing console. TOP RIGHT: Don Zientara (left) and Seth Martin setting up the new mixing console. 3OTTOM LEFT: (left to right) Joey Picuri, Seth Martin, and Don wiring the twenty four tracks. BOTTOM RIGHT: Joey Picuri. Photos by Jeff Nelson.

Jim Spellman, High Back Chairs, 1990.
Photo by Charles Steck.

Jim Spellman

High Back Chairs - Velocity Girl

We recorded the first High Back Chairs album at Inner Ear largely during overnight sessions. It was my first time in a real studio and I was very intimidated. Jeff Nelson is, of course, a legend who had made a bunch of legendary records, and Charles Steck was very experienced as well. Peter was the leader, and of course the legendary producer Ted Niceley was the most intimidating of all . . . both as Fugazi's producer and as a member of Tommy Keene's band.

But Don Z. was an immediate ally. He treated me as a peer from the first moment I met him. He was respectful and supportive and ALWAYS willing to answer questions and show me how things work.

A short time later Velocity Girl recorded the *My Forgotten Favorite* single there. We had a lot of wild recording ideas and he always took our ideas seriously (no matter how misguided) and tried to help us accomplish what we were aiming to do.

A few years later I had a little eight-track studio in my basement. When I was setting it up, Don was extremely helpful with guidance and selling me some of his old gear, cheap. Always, always, always encouraging.

Don always seemed to wear flip-flops in the studio, so when I started my little studio I got a pair as a tribute. Now, for better or worse, I wear flip-flops all the time . . . I blame Don.

High Back Chairs

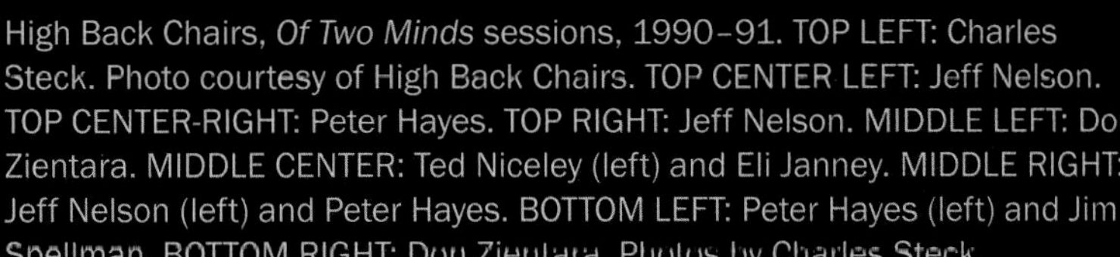

High Back Chairs, *Of Two Minds* sessions, 1990–91. TOP LEFT: Charles Steck. Photo courtesy of High Back Chairs. TOP CENTER LEFT: Jeff Nelson. TOP CENTER-RIGHT: Peter Hayes. TOP RIGHT: Jeff Nelson. MIDDLE LEFT: Don Zientara. MIDDLE CENTER: Ted Niceley (left) and Eli Janney. MIDDLE RIGHT: Jeff Nelson (left) and Peter Hayes. BOTTOM LEFT: Peter Hayes (left) and Jim Spellman. BOTTOM RIGHT: Don Zientara. Photos by Charles Steck.

Peter Hayes, High Back Chairs, 1990.
Photo by Charles Steck.

Peter Hayes

High Back Chairs

Lots of popular music is created by separating the musician from the music. But Inner Ear doesn't attract songwriting teams with celebrity producers. The Chairs' songs were pretty well hammered out by the time we got to the studio. Don was hands-off during tracking, and Ted and Eli brought in great ideas and enhancements during preproduction, overdubs, and mixing.

As any producer will attest, creativity and spontaneity can be time-consuming to capture. We were spending Dischord's money, so we did 99 percent of the songwriting, rehearsing, and demo-ing in the basement. Tracking didn't feel too different from rehearsing.

Amanda MacKaye

Desiderata - Routineers - Bed Maker

I was fortunate to be young and impressionable in the early years of the punk scene in DC. It was a time of curiosity and learning how to make our own way; to determine how to overcome and get around obstacles to our goals. The people around me were making music and planting seeds that I could do this too.

When I was in my first band, Desiderata (actually my second, but the Headaches never made it into the studio back in '79), we were able to record, professionally, in a studio. Of course, I don't think we ever said it that way, we just said we were "going to the studio." I use the term "able to record" because 1) we had a goal to do this, 2) we had access to both studios and engineers, and 3) we had all grown up witnessing our friends, older siblings, etc., go record in a studio; it was a completely natural progression of events. In its lifetime, Desiderata recorded with Barrett Jones at Laundry Room, WGNS with Geoff Turner, and Don Zientara at Inner Ear Studio.

Desiderata recorded with Don in the summer of 1991. This wasn't my first introduction to Don or even my first time being at Inner Ear. This session was pretty soon after Don moved the studio out of his house. My brothers Alec and Ian had both recorded with Don at Inner Ear and so had bands I was close to like Lünch Meat, Shudder to Think, and Swiz. But this was the first time I had worked with Don and it made an impression that guides my musicianship still. I went on to record with Don at Inner Ear with Jury Rig, the Routineers, and Chimp Suit.

Since the announcement of Inner Ear closing, there has been much said about its importance and some have even used the word "sacred" when describing the space that Don built. Though I am heartbroken about the closure, sacred is the not word that comes to mind about what we are saying goodbye to. The word I choose is: safe. We are losing a professional recording studio that was approachable and inviting for anyone.

As a woman and a musician who is primarily self-taught, and led by her gut, Don's "come as you are" vibe is empowering. Booking time with him was never intimidating and the sessions were completely inclusive. When working with Don and Inner Ear, I always felt heard and empowered to participate. It never mattered that I didn't know an octave from a note or a guitar head from an amp; nor did I know anything about Marshall, Vox, or Fender. I was treated as a valuable part of the band and an equal contributor to the experience. That is what Don and Inner Ear taught me.

As a vocalist who doesn't also play an instrument, recording is often a very vulnerable position. Often you are by yourself listening to the band through headphones and trying to feel connected to a song that was recorded some other time. Additionally, you might also be on view like a fish in an aquarium, when you are trying to nail your lyrics. There is a lot of trust involved with all of this, which is why when you find a space and an engineer that mesh with you and your band, you tend to stick with it. The layout of Inner Ear and Don's warm and affable nature were able to simultaneously honor the necessary separation for clean sounds and the critical "team effort" approach to get my vocals done. Hearing Don's voice at the end of a take is soothing, first and foremost, but his regard for me as a musician made me trust his gentle "Let's give this one another take and see where we are."

Furthermore, though the tide is shifting, when working with sound engineers, women musicians rarely see themselves reflected in recording studios or live venues. For the most part, I have been fortunate to have not encountered issues about being the only woman in the room when recording, but that doesn't mean I have been immune to the feeling of a bunch of men giving me notes on my performance or worse—being disenfranchised from my art. Inner Ear offered such an open book to "how things work," and also, "How would YOU like this to go?" As I got to know Don over the years, I learned that he taught himself about recording and built his own gear; he doesn't regard his skill or knowledge as his, per se. To me, this is the essence of Inner Ear: no ego.

All these years later, I still encounter the barriers that women in music have to get around, but they are less troublesome to me than the barriers of inequity in the world of studio recording. I fear that the curtain of mystery about recording studios that Don and Inner Ear lifted is being drawn closed again. Those of us who are not gearheads or who make music for ourselves will be at a disadvantage when entering new spaces because we likely won't speak the language, and then the power is shifted. Music becomes business.

In the time I spent at Inner Ear over the past thirty years, I never took advantage of my opportunity to learn to use the console, but I always had a seat there. Don Z. and Inner Ear encouraged in me that because I play music, therefore I am a musician; regardless of if I make records or play to hundreds of people. Reinforcing in me that in the true DIY manner, we aren't just supposed to do it for ourselves, we are supposed to lift as we climb and never forget where we were. As I embark on making new music and recording again, I am holding fast to the lessons learned in that safe space where I was considered an equal player. Even if I don't know the proper vocabulary (yet), I expect to be heard when I say, "No effects on my vocals." This is *my* voice, *I* decide if I want to make any changes.

Ian F. Svenonius

Nation of Ulysses - The Make-Up - Chain and the Gang - Escape-ism

Inner Ear Studio was the site used for the recording of both of Ulysses's proper studio records. It was a fun place full of laughs. Ian and Don were a fantastic team who indulged ideas and creativity but always kept things on track and spirits high. Making a record with the two of them, one felt part of a mission that was important, and they invested each with adrenaline and purpose. Inner Ear was a legend to me as a youngster, as it was the name on the credits of all the Dischord records. These records often featured snippets of laughter, inside jokes, etc., and so the mood of Inner Ear was rightly assumed to be a clubhouse for an esoteric gang of cutups and nonconformists.

Don's studio was the home to all the radical groups in DC of all stripes, until home-recording technology became the norm. This technology cut costs for musicians, of course, but there's something to be said for the hothouse environment that a studio like Inner Ear provided.

Steve Gamboa

Nation of Ulysses - The Make-Up

I think that the environment one is performing in, whether practice space, studio, or stage, will always have a different effect on the experience of playing music. It might be a bit drastic to suggest that creativity can be snatched away going from practice to studio space, but I would say it does have an influence on recording, simply because the studio is always going to be a lot less familiar than your practice space. Making the studio environment as comfortable and intimate for the musicians comes down to a few elements, most importantly the house engineer/producer and their ability to understand where you are coming from musically and what the band is trying to achieve with the recording. And these are what made Inner Ear special in my opinion. Because Don had such a long history and relationship with Dischord bands prior to us recording there for our first session in 1991, by the time we made a record at Inner Ear, Don already had a good understanding of the Dischord sound and vibe. Not to mention Inner Ear already had such a reputation within DC hardcore history that we were pretty stoked to be a part of its legacy. Don welcomed us in as part of the family from jump, and that, alongside his professional guidance and infinite patience, really had a big impact on our recording experiences there. It's been a good thirty years since I last set foot in Inner Ear, but I still have fond memories of the legendary Z-Man with his big white trainers, hiked-up jeans, and corny-ass jokes. Nuff Respect to Don Z. and Inner Ear Studio!

Arika Casebolt

Circus Lupus

How to Be Don Zientara

First, be tall. Be so tall and substantial that it's impossible to be unaffected by such a presence. Soften your movements and your signature vast lope, and duck a little into doorways just to make others comfortable. Be beyond kind. Remain patient, even in the face of all sorts of very young, very obnoxious, and immature musicians. Intuit how best to smooth out the path for the best possible result for the finished product. Be so soothing a presence that you can ease tensions in the whole emotional environment of the exceptional Inner Ear Studio. Imbue everything you touch with swiftly practiced hands, with skill and ease. Be incredibly thoughtful and always find ways to best elevate a song.

Have deeply personal, private pain. Remain stoic. Be reserved. Be incredibly funny in a very sweet, paternal way. When you make a joke and notice someone loving it, keep repeating the punch line to the point of silliness. Make the "Oops, I forgot the room mic was on" joke a lot and at everyone's expense and make it hilarious every time. Adore liquorice allsorts candy, which is gross. Don't talk much. Listen and be tuned in to whatever project is before you. Watch the kids. Discover how everything shakes out in the best way, and guide musicians graciously and with real advice, and only when asked.

And when you lope across the hallway during a weird little band's recording session—because your legs are twice the average length of everyone else's, it's only about a four-lope trip—and you find a frightened, inexperienced drummer standing crumbling in the hallway, put down the piece of hardware you're holding. Stand next to the aforementioned weeping girl, who is looking at Hot Snakes album covers and unable to stem the flow of tears. Because you are Don Zientara, be the only person in the building to bother comforting her. Tell her the very kind words that saved her in really bad times—words she still carries with her every single day.

Being Don Zientara, you have been a lighthouse in the dark for countless musicians, directly and indirectly, and a truly generous part of a historic musical movement. Be admired and adored, whether you like it or not. Enjoy your retirement to the fullest, and enjoy being an actual icon, because that's who you are.

Inner Ear Studio
PUSH

Living room. Photo by Antonia Tricarico, 2021.

Living room and kitchen. Photo by Antonia Tricarico, 2021.

Living room LP covers on the wall. Photo by Antonia Tricarico, 2021.

FUGAZI
ASSALTI
MARTEDI
20
GIUGNO
INIZIA PRIMA DEL TRAMONTO
ORE
18.00
CENTRO SOCIALE OCCUPATO AUTOGESTITO
FORTE PRENESTINO

Control room. Photo by Antonia Tricarico, 2021

Live room. Photo by Antonia Tricarico, 2021.

BANDS

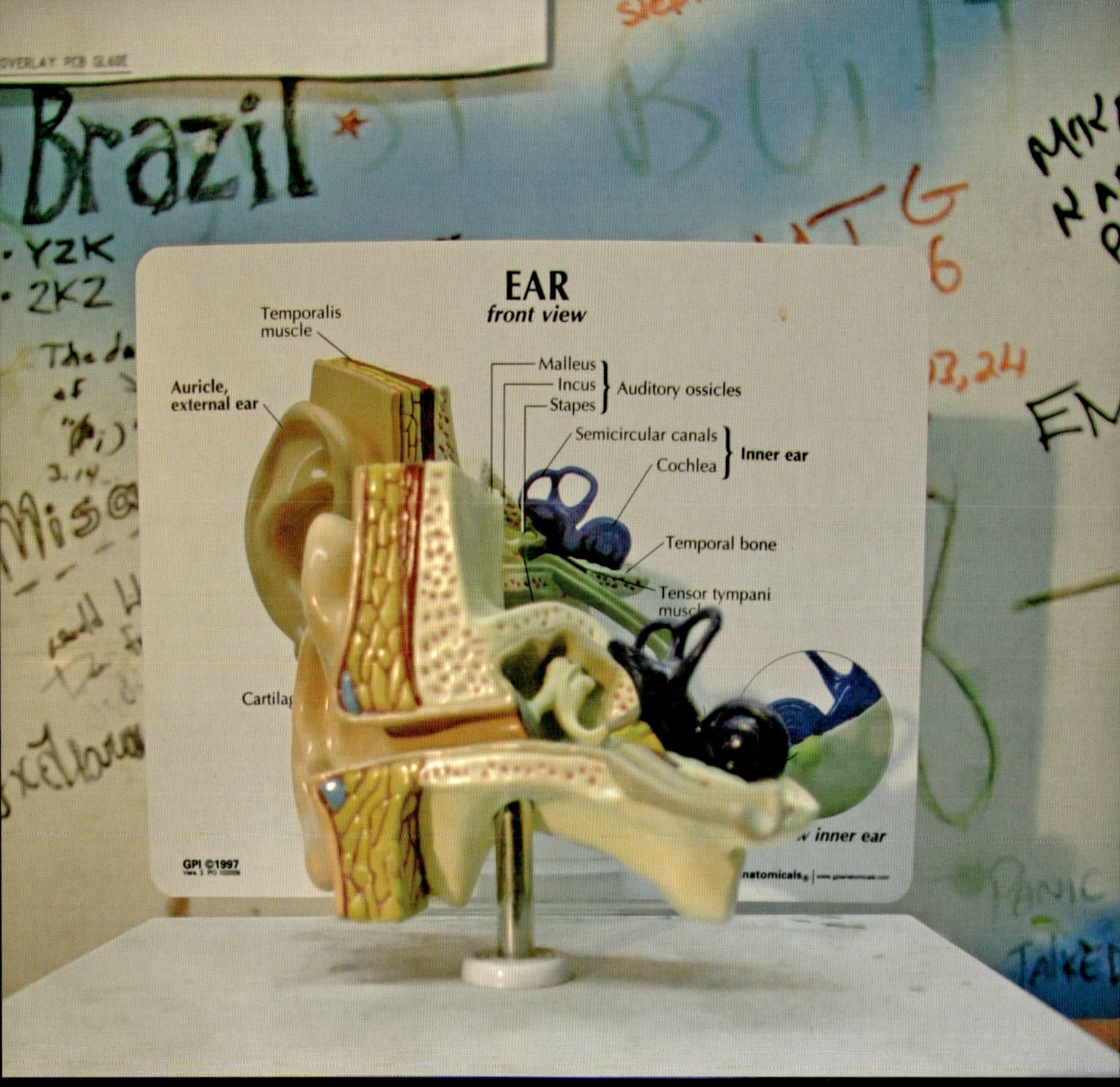

Ear model by GPI Anatomicals, given to Don Zientara as a gift. Photo by Antonia Tricarico, 2021.

Seth Lorinczi

Circus Lupus - The Golden Bears - The Quails

I spent a fair bit of time at Inner Ear over the years, beginning in 1988, when it was just Don's basement. I was seventeen then and it was my first "real" experience in a studio. And while I'd eventually become obsessed with audio gear—the McIntosh tube amp behind the board was a touchstone—it wasn't the "stuff" that drew me in: it was Don. He was quietly charismatic, curious, and genuinely kind. It's an unusual combination, especially in the world of recording, and it always left an impression on me.

Standout moments? Recording the first Circus Lupus album with Eli Janney at the controls; glancing into the control room as we tracked "Pacifier" and seeing Jennifer Ballard dancing along. It was just so thrilling, the sense that we were making something stranger and cooler and better than we'd even imagined.

More weirdness: A year or so later, Joan Jett took an interest in us. She'd gotten big into Fugazi and Lungfish, and someone told her to check us out at CBGB. So it was arranged that she and her producer, Kenny Laguna, would fly down to DC to do a single with us.

It was pretty surreal. Joan definitely wasn't "technical" in terms of making suggestions; she was more of a vibe master. We were thrilled at the thought that we were the first band she'd "produced" since the Germs, but when we asked her about recording *GI*, all she could really remember was what kind of drugs everyone was on.

Kenny was a complete trip. He'd come up in '60s bubblegum groups: "I was in the 1910 Fruitgum Company!" he proudly told us. Crickets. And though he made lots of suggestions, I don't think we actually followed any of them. Like, fast-walking past the control room door, he'd bark, "Hey, Don, slap some 10k on those vocals!" and then just keep walking. (I don't think Don slapped any 10k on the vocals.) Or, trying to goad us into a better take: "Come on, guys! Let's fry this turkey while it's hot!"

But really, it was a truly magical couple of days. Some people thought Joan was only there to establish her "Original Riot Grrrl" cred, but I felt she was truly genuine, and above all an absolute music fan. Kenny too: maybe he was trying to butter me up, but he said my bass playing reminded him of Leigh Gorman, the guy from Bow Wow Wow (who's an absolutely insane player). I feel really warmly toward both of them to this day.

And Don? In the midst of all the energy and weirdness, he was a total rock, equanimous and chill. It made what could have been a freakish situation really stress-free and fun. A peak experience, and one I'm still grateful for today.

Kathleen Hanna (Bikini Kill, the Julie Ruin, Le Tigre) interviewed by Antonia Tricarico

January 11, 2021

Antonia Tricarico: How did you find out about Don's studio?

Kathleen Hanna: Bikini Kill played DC Space, I think in June 1991. Ian MacKaye was at the show. He came up afterward and said he loved the show. It was strange for us because we had just been on a tour where men were throwing stuff at us and being like, "Fuck you, bitches, show us your tits," right? So it was definitely odd to have a white guy come up and say, "I love what you're doing." And he seemed excited.

Tricarico: I would've had the same reaction, coming from the late-'70s feminist collective and playing drums in a band. So all the men were saying, "Oh, that's incredible. A woman playing drums." I understand the feeling. That does remind me of my youth in common with other women living the same situation, on different continents, in a different time.

Hanna: Yeah. So at that time I listened to Fugazi. I listened to Minor Threat, Rites of Spring, a lot of DC stuff, but I didn't recognize Ian. And I thought he was a creep, or he was one of those guys who was like, "Oh, I love girls in bands." You're so used to being treated poorly that you automatically assume when a man walks up to you that it's not going to be good. So when he was like, "Oh, you're so great!" and he was acting normal, I was kind of shocked. Then he asked me what we had recorded, and we only had a demo tape that we recorded on reel-to-reel, with this guy Pat Maley in Olympia. I'd only recorded in people's basements, garages, on four-track cassette or eight-track reel-to-reel. That was the extent of my recording experience, although I did take a recording class where I did eight-track TEAC Tascam reel-to-reel, so I had some sort of experience in the studio. So Ian said, "My friend Don has a recording studio, and since you guys only have a demo, we should record right away because you never know."

Tricarico: Yes, a band may dissolve as quickly as it was formed or totally change the sound, the energy.

Hanna: It's like somebody can get pissed at someone, and your band breaks up the next day. Songs will be lost forever. You just never make it to the studio because you don't have money. So he had a sense of urgency like, *I have to get this young band into the studio.* And I walked away from him thinking, *That guy is trying to kill us, he's going to take us to the woods and murder us.* And Tobi and Kathi: "Oh my God, that was Ian MacKaye. I can't believe you were talking to him." And I was like, "Wait, the guy from for Minor Threat was just talking to me? Oh, that's so cool." We couldn't record over the summer, because Kathi left right after the show and went to Europe. And then we stayed around for the summer and then when we moved to DC—I think that's when we recorded.

Tricarico: Do you have specific memories about the recording? Did you have some kind of feeling about Don, the way he was doing his job?

Hanna: At the time I was so insecure and so terrified that I wasn't thinking about anybody else. Which is what you are when you're twenty-two, twenty-three, twenty-four, or whatever we were. But I remember thinking he was the adult. And he was making sure everything was getting captured. I immediately trusted him and knew that he just treated us like people, he didn't treat us weird. And I could tell that he and Ian had such a rapport with each other that it felt like they were doing the project together. It didn't feel like it was Don, it felt like it was Don and Ian.

Stills of Kathleen Hanna from video interview with Antonia Tricarico.

Don was the person moving the buttons, and Ian was communicating with us more because we didn't know Don and we were kind of scared. I think Don probably wasn't even that much older. I mean, I don't know how old he is now.

Tricarico: He is seventy-three.

Hanna: He's like twenty years, eighteen, fifteen years older than me. He was like thirty-five, forty. Yeah, it's not like he's ancient. But to us, he didn't dress like a punk. So we were like, "Oh, Ian has this relationship with this businessman?"

Tricarico: So the recording took place at Inner Ear's new location, not in the basement. For you all, as a band, it was more professional. Maybe more intimidating?

Hanna: So no, this is not in a basement. This is like a nice studio, I think it had like kind of a roundish control center, as I recall. And he just set us up in this main room. Yeah. [For our previous recording], we played a party and we left our stuff set up and then the guy mic'd it and then we recorded it. We were very freaked out at Inner Ear that we were going to do the wrong thing. Say the wrong thing.

Tricarico: During my research for this book, I couldn't find many women who were studio engineers. I've seen some at live shows running the monitors.

Hanna: Well, I'm just in the process of hiring people to do front-of-house and monitors for a tour.

Tricarico: Oh, that's fantastic. Did you ever search for a studio that was run by a woman? Do you think that would make you more comfortable?

Hanna: Yeah. When I was in my next band, Le Tigre, from like 1999 to 2007, it took us four years to find a female engineer in New York. But at that time it didn't feel like an option. "Hey, are there any female-run studios, any female engineers and female producers?" We couldn't do that, and we were so focused on getting girls to come to our shows that recording was an afterthought for us. Our whole band was based on live. So for us, recording at that point, it just happened. Like, we weren't thinking, *How do we get the money to record? How do we do this? How do we get a label?* We were just trying to stay afloat. *How do we get money to get to the next place? Where are we going to sleep?* So the thought of, you know, *Oh, I want to record with a woman*, was like, *Yeah, I'm going to be a professional gymnast*.

Tricarico: Let's talk about creativity during the process of making music, from the practice space to the recording studio. How do you keep the integrity in your music when you step out from your practice space and go into a studio? I have been in the studio once myself with my band in Italy. I was the only woman. I had the feeling that they wanted to control me as much as they could. Also, the sound engineer looked at me like I was from another planet.

Hanna: "Oh, you should get more kick, more snare . . ."

Tricarico: Yeah! Did you have that feeling recording at Inner Ear?

Hanna: No, no. As I said, I was nervous. I felt thankful because we didn't have the money to afford that, and the fact that a musician that I liked, like Ian, had set this free recording up for us—I just wanted to do a good job, and I knew that because there were men listening and headphones, I was performing for them, right? To a certain extent. And so there's a cutesiness I think I was trying to have that I might have not had if there was a woman on the other end who I felt was my peer. But I didn't. They weren't condescending. They weren't rude. I only found out later that it was odd to have a good experience, because later I recorded a solo album, went to master it, and had the mastering guys tell me to go get some coffee. And I was *paying* them and they wouldn't listen to me.

Tricarico: How was the experience of recording with Don?

Hanna: Don was like . . . he just disappeared. Kind of. I felt like he was trying to get the best performance out of us. It wasn't about his ego, and it wasn't about him telling us what to do. He just gave us space to make what we were making. The thing is, I didn't realize the art of recording, even though I'd taken a class in it and when I sat in front of the board, I knew exactly what to do because I've read the manual right because I wasn't a douchey guy who's like, *I'm not going to read the manual, I'm just going to . . .* I read the manual and I had a good time. It felt like painting and I enjoyed it. But I kind of forgot all about that. That one class I had taken a couple of years before, and when we were in there, I was just trying to be present for the songs, and to get the emotion across, and to not be too nervous, and to just worry about maintaining my throat, and that kind of stuff, because the songs are kind of athletic. So I felt like, *I want to do the best I can.* But also I didn't see Ian, I didn't look up to him. I did look up to him much later and he became a mentor, but he was just a guy. I felt I was definitely in an environment where I could speak up for myself, but I didn't understand the recording equipment.

Tricarico: Were you afraid that your work could be jeopardized by the studio's technical aspect?

Hanna: Yeah! I felt a little lost, like it was my job to perform and their job to do that part. And for many years in that band, the same thing, we had the same attitude, or at least I did. That recording was taking a snapshot of who we were as a band. But what you don't realize when you think that way is that a snapshot isn't neutral—who's taking the snapshot? What kind of camera? Is it color? Is it black-and-white? How do you feel when you're being photographed? Are you a part of the process? Did you choose to be photographed? Like all of those different things . . . The recording's an art form and you can record something and make it sound really live or like it's a whole new expression.

And I think for a long time in our band, because of financial constraints and because of our psychological well-being, because of how we were treated often, we didn't have time to think about the art of it, even though we were listening to the Slits's *Cut* and talking about the recording. Yeah, we weren't thinking about it in terms of us. We were just like, *How do we get in the studio and make something as quick and cheap as possible?* It wasn't until toward the end of the band, the last record and the singles, all of our singles, and It was really working with Joan Jett, that change that I saw. *Oh, there's this possibility of making art*, but it worked for us then even though there were two men who were mediating the sound. It was a high-quality recording. We always felt our live show was the strongest part of our band. And so we wanted it to sound like a live show. We didn't want it to be perfect.

Tricarico: So you did get that from the Inner Ear recording . . . ?

Hanna: Yes. And they didn't put a shit-ton of reverb on my voice, I knew what I wanted. I think I said a tiny bit of reverb and a little slapback. That's what I always asked for. I was like, "Just a little bit of this, a little bit of that," but it was very raw.

Tricarico: It was a pleasure talking to you, hopefully we'll meet again at your shows. Thank you for your contribution.

Hanna: Thank you for including me.

Myra Power

Slant 6 - Tarot Bolero

What a magical, fascinating time to actually get to record our Slant 6 songs at Inner Ear with Don and Ian. Don was so kind and patient. I was incredibly shy and uncertain about how to record vocals. Ian really helped me figure out how to drop some of the lyrics to "Poison Arrows Shot at Heroes" so that the song fit more together. We laughed that I wanted to ramble on like a David Johansen.

Shelby Cinca

Frodus - Decahedron

My first Inner Ear experience was when Don Zientara recorded my band Frodus back in December of 1993 while we were still in high school. With our own money from cassette and 7" profits and borrowed cash from friends and Ian MacKaye, we went in to record our debut album. At a prior meeting with Don when reviewing our 7" recording plans, he had drawn a parallel with the spastic energy of Rites of Spring, which was quite the honor.

When the session began, we came in well-practiced but slightly nervous. After a train wreck of a first day, we started over and Don helped us find our groove with his subtle nudges about what we should focus on. His ability to create a calm atmosphere for creativity was unparalleled. I distinctly remember his serving of Spam on crackers and strong coffee in very pleasing 1950s-style diner mugs—one of which I borrowed from the studio back in 1993 that I still have in my possession.

My memory flickers between standing in the live room and noticing the color splashes of art and the patterns on the amplifiers, to the very dry-sounding vocal booth, and lastly to the control room. The mix is when it all came together and Don weaved the sonic soup we made into a focused sound-painting of our frenetic punk (which we dubbed "spazzcore").

Throughout the session, Don was like a Zen master guiding us and letting the session go down its own path when the flow was there. Despite me hearing some distinct Inner Ear sonic characteristics of the room, what came out of the speakers was definitely the best realization of us and our energy at the time.

Inner Ear was an extension of Don himself: the relaxing atmosphere, the focus, the creativity—all coming into play as only Don Z. could do. It is a space that will be sorely missed yet remembered fondly by many.

I raise my mug to Don Z., aka "Donzie"!

TOP LEFT: Decahedron in the Inner Ear alley during their 2005 session. (Left to right) Shelby Cinca, Jason Hamacher, and Jake Brown. Photo by Mark Beemer. TOP RIGHT: "A picture of a mug I 'borrowed' from the studio in 1993 that I still have. I thought it was very classic American diner and a strong memory of my first Inner Ear experience. Coffee and Don offering us Spam and crackers as a snack!" —Shelby Cinca. BOTTOM: (left to right) Shelby Cinca, Jason Hamacher, and Jake Brown. Photo by Mark Beemer.

Jason Hamacher

Frodus - Decahedron - Battery - Combatwoundedveteran

I met Don Zientara at Inner Ear Studio in the fall of 1993. My band Frodus had just gotten the test pressings of our first EP recorded that summer at WGNS Studios in Arlington. We were beyond excited to make a record, so I tracked down a few DC music legends, introduced my teen self, and let them know Frodus had recorded. None of these people had heard of the band, knew who we were, or what we sounded like. We hadn't even played a real show. I was enthusiastically seventeen.

I got Inner Ear's number out of the phone book and called one day after school.

"Hello, Inner Ear."

"Hey! My name is Jason and I play drums in a band called Frodus. We live in the area and just recorded a 7"."

"Hey, Jason, I'm Don. That's great you guys recorded! Why don't you come by the studio sometime so we can listen to the songs?" I couldn't believe Don Zientara personally answered the phone. He had just recorded Fugazi's *In on the Kill Taker* and Circus Lupus's *Solid Brass*. I was shocked he invited us to stop by. Everything about Inner Ear was iconic, from the name to the logo to the legacy and even the location. The song "Weenie Beenie" on the first Foo Fighters album is named after the hot dog stand around the corner from Inner Ear. With such a legendary roster of music coming out of there, Inner Ear seemed more creative incubator than recording studio.

A few days later, Shelby (guitarist and singer in Frodus) and I were speeding toward Inner Ear leaving the doldrums of suburbia behind. We had no idea what to expect and were confused by Don's invitation. We knew nothing about him aside from music and hearing his voice on Minor Threat and Swiz songs. I parked in front of the Inner Ear sign and rang the doorbell. An older man with wildly long legs wearing OP shorts and flip-flops answered the door. With exuberance rivaling Will Ferrell's anchorman, we were greeted with a big, "Hey, guys, I'm Don Zientara. Come on in and let me show you around!"

We followed Don down a dark hallway into a room with some cabinets and a few couches. "Here's the lounge where bands hang out. We've got a little kitchen over here if people want tea or coffee . . ." We were stunned by the wall of album covers: Minor Threat, Soulside, Gray Matter, Embrace, Scream, King Face, Happy Flowers . . . This place was responsible for music that altered the course of my life, and the guy who ran it was inconceivably hospitable. I leaned over to Shelby and whispered, "Dude, this is insane!"

We left the lounge and walked down a hallway covered in more albums, artwork, CDs, articles, and awards. He showed us the live room, vocal booth, drum riser, and ended the tour in the control room. We were beyond impressed and seriously overwhelmed.

"So, guys, let's hear this recording!" I handed him the test pressing. He placed it on a turntable, pushed a few buttons, patched a few cables, and before we understood what was happening, Don was blasting Frodus through Inner Ear's massive reference speakers. I couldn't believe it. He listened intently switching between speaker sets and providing technical feedback and constructive commentary.

All of the insight, attention, and generosity from such an influential audio engineer was hard for me to grasp. So much so, I was concerned Don thought he had *recorded* Frodus. Why would he devote so much time and energy to a couple of random teenagers?

After listening to side A, Don declared, "That sounds pretty good. Now let's listen to something else for comparison." Shelby and I looked at each other, silently wondering what he was going to choose. He pulled a small box out of the hallway closet, opened it, and began threading a tape machine.

I nervously whispered to Shelby, "Does he think he recorded us?" Shelby shrugged in confusion.

Don finished setting up the tape machine and then turned around: "Okay, guys, let's listen."

"What are we listening to?" I asked.

"It's something we recorded a few years ago," and he casually handed me the Rites of Spring *All Through a Life* master tape. Seriously? Rites of Spring??!!!! Things were officially out of control. He played a few songs, switching between speakers, talking us through technical aspects: song spacing, tones, mix, all kinds of things we weren't really thinking about. It was incredibly surreal listening to Rites of Spring with the guy who recorded them as an exercise to learn about ourselves. We still weren't sure if Don thought he had recorded our songs and we were too embarrassed to say anything. After the impromptu Rites of Spring party, we exchanged contact info, thanked him for everything, and left Inner Ear in shock.

We sat in my truck reeling from the experience. "Can you believe that just happened? What the hell! We'll record here someday, I know we will." We drove back to Springfield, Virginia, full of excitement and ambition.

Frodus recorded our first album just a few months later at Inner Ear with Don. It was an incredible experience that changed my life. Looking back, the true magic of Inner Ear wasn't found in the control room but in Don's ability to encourage, inspire, and empower kids through their own music, and for that I'm eternally grateful.

Giovanna Cacciola & Agostino Tilotta

Uzeda - Bellini

Although we have been there several times and never recorded there, it is still a trauma for us to think that Inner Ear Studio will be closed forever. In those walls, all the enthusiasms, joys, and frustrations will remain imprinted, translated, and immortalized in the history of music by dozens of bands, the most acclaimed and famous in Washington, DC, who played and recorded in that place, loved with exclusive passion by Fugazi, a place invented by the gentleness, elegance, passion, generosity, and humility of a man whose greatness goes far beyond the role of a sound engineer, a man named Don Zientara. It was 1995 when I contacted him, after having obtained his telephone number at Dischord, to ask him if he wanted to come to Catania, Sicily, to record thirteen local bands in an analog studio in our city.

Don's open availability answered my skepticism, and he gladly accepted my invitation, with the only condition being that he would bring a studio assistant with him. I accepted, and so I also met Joey "P" Picuri. They stayed in Catania for three weeks, recording every day for two good weeks. It was a fantastic period of harmony that drew relationships of sincere friendship and pure dialogue. The people in the bands listened to Don's directions and advice, and Don satisfied their requests, putting them at ease and encouraging them when excited and intimidated. In the same year, the recording sessions became a CD entitled *Lapilli*. Even today those musicians, now grown up, parents, architects, lawyers, graphic designers, postmen, etc., always remember those days spent with Don Zientara, "the tallest and kindest sound engineer in the world." I saw Joey P again that same year, at a show that Giovanna and I organized in Catania with Fugazi and Uzeda. Joey was Fugazi's sound man. And with Giovanna I saw Don again in the USA, at his home, and in Inner Ear in

Arlington, and at the Middle East in Boston where he flew to see a Uzeda show with Shellac. Our friendship has always been pure crystal, based on mutual respect and affectionate esteem. Although separated by gigantic oceans and immense distances, our relationship is always fueled by a universal love that breaks down barriers, borders, pandemics, and wars. We love and will continue to love Don forever and ever.

Eric Axelson

The Dismemberment Plan - Statehood

Early on, every record we loved seemed to be made at Inner Ear with Don Zientara engineering. So when we finally had enough songs to record, we nervously called up and got on the calendar. Not sure why, but in the weeks leading up to our session we'd decided that a guy with a name like Don Zientara was likely a super-tough old-school punk who lived in a studio, chain-smoking and grunting orders: "Wrong—do it again!" The day finally came, we pulled into the alley next to the studio, and bounding out of the door was a super-tall dude in flip-flops, short surf shorts, a surf T-shirt, and glasses: "Hi, I'm Don!" He was the warmest and most inviting person—it didn't matter that we didn't look like (early days two of us looked halfway between grunge and the Grateful Dead, one was clearly in a frat, and Travis looked like he might help with your taxes) or sound like (*!* was an exercise in ADD and caffeine abuse) anything going on in DC in 1994. We were weirdos going on our own bizarre trip, and Don was all about helping us stay on the path.

We were brand new to recording, and Don answered the thousands of questions we had, let us try unorthodox stuff, and steered us away from the REALLY bad ideas. I'm not sure we ever got comfortable that first session—we were too young and neurotic—but as we came back again and again, Inner Ear felt like home. We'd pore over the photos and album covers on the walls, sit in the corner messing with the hundreds of puzzles in the studio while each other tracked, try to sneak a nap on the sofa in a pile of self-inflicted pretzel crumbs, and keep popping back into the control room with more questions. Later on we found out that some local bands and labels knew about us because Don would mention us to others who'd come in to record. For a band with a metal name, this made for a softer entry.

Over the years I think I was part of seven full-lengths that were made at (or at least partially made at) Inner Ear: the first four Dismemberment Plan records, the first Maritime, the last Gena Rowlands Band, the only Statehood. And it was home to the recordings of many friends who lived near DC (Smart Went Crazy, Branch Manager, Most Secret Method . . . and tons of others) or traveled to work there (Promise Ring . . . who destroyed us in a four-on-four basketball game during a break in the *Very Emergency* sessions; Braid . . . who slept on my floor while tracking *Frame & Canvas*). My life has been so much better because of the music I was able to make, and the music others made, at Inner Ear Studio.

Steve Cummings

The Dismemberment Plan

We recorded *!* over two sessions—separated by a few months if I recall. My two enduring memories of my time at Inner Ear were that Don had a nearly endless amount of jokes with drummers being the punch line. The second was more essential—about that great studio and what it meant to young bands. These sessions were our first serious recordings,

The Dismemberment Plan

The Dismemberment Plan, *Change* session, 2001. TOP LEFT: Don Zientara. TOP CENTER: Eric Axelson. TOP RIGHT: J. Robbins. BOTTOM LEFT: Travis Morrison. BOTTOM LEFT-CENTER: Joe Easley. BOTTOM RIGHT-CENTER: Joe Easley (left) and J. Robbins. Photos by Jason Caddell. BOTTOM RIGHT: Jason Caddell. Photo courtesy of the Dismemberment Plan.

and even though I was a poseur and bit aloof, I wanted to do my best for the boys. Don was in the main booth and setting up drum mics and asked me what I wanted out of the recording. I was at a loss, and essentially asked, "What do you think?" He wasn't having that and patiently made it clear that it was our music and my drumming and I should be thinking and pushing for the sound I wanted. So here was a studio, available for young no-name bands at a fair price and flexible to allow new producers (heya, Chad Clark) to come in and work the control room—that alone was a tremendous resource at the time for new bands to launch, but he also got us thinking much more deeply about what it was we wanted to do with the music. He made us at least pretend to be professionals by treating us and the music with respect. Listening to *!* now reminds me how many decisions we made were dead wrong, but that tinny frenetic album really launched the band. I don't think anything the Plan produced after those days happens without Don and Inner Ear.

Jem Cohen

Filmmaker and Photographer

"Submarine"

If you're going to be stuck in a submarine, you'd better have a good commander and a solid engine room. You don't expect windows, though you will long for them. Somewhere in California or the woods upstate there's a studio with sun-drenched wraparound windows and crafted wooden ceilings and gorgeous lamps, but this isn't that studio. I can barely remember the neighborhood like I can barely remember most industrial strips. Inner Ear was a good name for it: a chamber, isolated, kind of secret. Don, in my experience, was so levelheaded that he became an enigma. After all, musicians are often anything but levelheaded, especially in the pressure chamber that is a recording session. So, in that context, calm competence might seem an anomaly, mysterious indeed. Maybe he *is* a mystery—how can a person stay so calm, so gentlemanly, so decent and amused, as deadlines loom and personalities swirl and doubts pile up and sometimes explode all around him? Would he ever crack? Not in my experience, but I was really only around for any length at Fugazi sessions, which were very intense, sometimes deranged, but mostly kind of civilized. And very funny.

As for the physical place, I never found it especially beautiful or aesthetically charged. It was a pocket of history, organized, lined with often ugly record covers, well-stocked with dumb games and puzzles—distractions that can keep someone from going insane while they wait for the amp sound to get right. I'm not a gear head so I can't say much about the equipment, but as the sessions I was at were all analog, my memories are marked by turning reels of one-inch tape with spinning metal hubs and the simultaneous solidity and irrevocability of analog recording. Limitations: terrifying but embraced, oddly comforting. You got the take, you got it; you burned it, it's gone. Nowhere to go but forward.

My memories from Inner Ear are mostly of shooting for *Instrument*. I'd borrowed some Hi8 video gear that I didn't know how to use well at all. I had my Super 8 too, to get footage with some juice, but it couldn't do sync sound. Aesthetics would have to be secondary—to the process, the truth of the long grind, the sonic discoveries, muttered curses and occasional exaltation. I had to make the video work, even though the image looked lifeless and ugly. Like it was shot in a submarine.

Fugazi, *Red Medicine* session, 1995. TOP LEFT: Joe Lally (left) and Brendan Canty. TOP RIGHT: track list. MIDDLE LEFT: Ian MacKaye. MIDDLE RIGHT: Guy Picciotto (front) and Brendan Canty. BOTTOM: listening to playback (left to right) Guy Picciotto, Joe Lally, Brendan Canty, and Ian MacKaye. Photos by Jem Cohen.

LEFT: Coriky, 2021. (Left to right) Joe Lally, Amy Farina, Don Zientara, and Ian MacKaye. Photo by Antonia Tricarico. RIGHT: Don (left) and Ian MacKaye at the Dag Nasty *Cold Heart* recording session, 2015. Photo by Michelle C. Roberts.

Amy Farina (The Warmers - The Evens - Coriky)

Derrick Decker
Branch Manager

I went, recorded, it was great, Don was cool, the end! 

Ron Winters
Blood Bats - Branch Manager

[*Text conversation between Ron and Antonia.*]

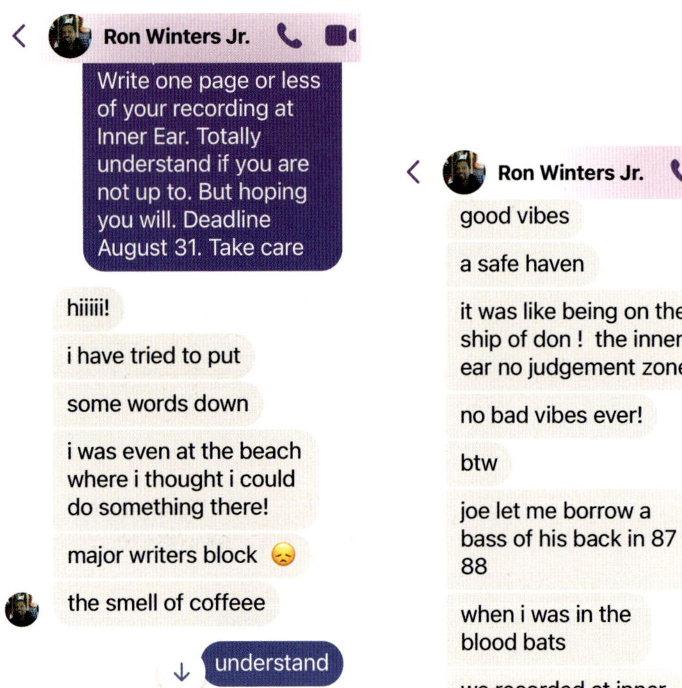

Ron Winters Jr.
good vibes
a safe haven
it was like being on the ship of don ! the inner ear no judgement zone
no bad vibes ever!
btw
joe let me borrow a bass of his back in 87 88
when i was in the blood bats
we recorded at inner ear then too

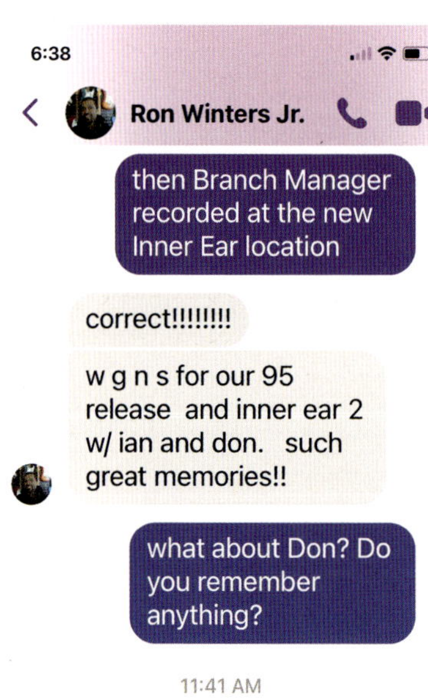

6:38
Ron Winters Jr.
then Branch Manager recorded at the new Inner Ear location
correct!!!!!!!!
w g n s for our 95 release and inner ear 2 w/ ian and don. such great memories!!
what about Don? Do you remember anything?
11:41 AM

11:41 AM
just being a super
person
no judgements
he is still the same as he is today!!
supportive but will say in the cans
"are you sure you don't want to do that one again?".
so he was super tuned in and had such wisdom on the sonics

Luca Mascini (aka Militant A)

Assalti Frontali

We were the underground Kings of Rome in the 1990s. Assalti Frontali (Frontal Assaults)—this is our name. And we assaulted the record industry on stages, in universities, and on the streets.

Every concert, every album, was a political statement. We sang for a movement that aimed to create cities that were just, free, and welcoming to all. Our base was the squat Forte Prenestino in the Centocelle district, in Rome's southeastern outskirts. An abandoned military fort with loopholes, arms squares, ditches, and underground cells, it had been occupied and revived by dozens of young people and activists in the area in 1986, with parties, assemblies, and films. It was a social gathering space for students and young people. There, we put on legendary concerts for as many as ten thousand people.

So many of the counterculture groups came to perform for us, and they made a point of stopping in Rome on their tours because the Forte Prenestino had a revolutionary vibe.

In 1991 and 1995, Assalti Frontali shared the stage with Mano Negra and Fugazi. Those concerts led us to Don Zientara, the legendary producer who created the sound of Washington, DC, and Dischord Records in his Inner Ear Studio, a sound that we loved despite our musical genre being rap.

We adored Don's gritty sound, as well as the imagery of cultural independence, of freedom, possibility, and innovation. In order to achieve our goals, we decided that Rome, too, needed a recording studio that was open to all independent bands. And it had to be the H.C. Musica Forte recording studio in Forte Prenestino. The market challenge was possible thanks to a top-notch (in our heads) space in a busy community center. And we knew who we wanted to inaugurate it: Don Zientara.

Our new album, *Conflitto*, was almost finished, with rap lyrics and hardcore music performed by Brutopop. We spent months preparing the walls with lime and sand, then fitting the rooms in one of the fort's cells with acoustic panels. We bet everything on a thirty-six-channel Amek Angela analog mixing board, dismissing the idea of a cheaper but too-cold digital mixer in pursuit of our dreams (and delusions of grandeur). A used Amek was being sold by a well-known studio in a good part of Rome. We didn't think it was perfect, but it was a good deal. We rented a van and went to collect the Amek with all of the proceeds from the previous year's concerts, as well as loans from close friends.

We quickly discovered that the channels were not working when we returned to the fort and reassembled the treasure with our childlike enthusiasm. There was nothing more that could be done—not a single channel functioned. They all were having issues.

We met with an engineer who had worked in the studio that sold us the mixing board, and he revealed the trick: the main desk had started with two Amek Angelas, and when one of them broke, they replaced it with the one from Studio B, and then sold the broken one to us. With a few friends, we returned to the studio and spoke with the owner. We were enraged. We stayed there for an entire afternoon, obstructing recording sessions. In the end, the guy admitted his mistake and compensated us with microphones, amplifiers, and main desk channels.

Our H.C. Musica Forte, however, remained a shambles. And the album had to come out. Everyone waited. Our dream was full of unexpected twists and turns. Building a studio was difficult enough, and then we encountered despicable, greedy people in unexpected places. But this was not always the case. Don Zientara agreed to travel all the way from Washington to save our album, along with the concept we represented.

In December of 1995, Don arrived in Rome. He had fifteen days to record, produce, and mix *Conflitto*'s ten tracks.

"Don, what do you want to see in Rome while you are here?" we asked when we picked him up at the airport.

"I'd just like to see your studio," he said. "We'll go out the last night." He didn't want anything to get in the way of his work. He refused to listen to any music other than ours.

We were all on edge once we entered the H.C. Would we really be able to do this? Don moved his big hands through our studio's tangle of wires, which he found "funny," with the electric current that came and went.

"Of course it's possible," he said, "so let's get started."

Informal, naive, and unusual, but also strict, serious, and orderly—Don left the house in his slippers in December, and while he worked, he exuded absolute calm and the assurance that everything would be fine. Beyond the technical specifications, he was most concerned with recording authenticity; his goal was to capture the spontaneity and naturalness of the voice and chords, and the groove, all of which he knew were essential ingredients in the success of a record.

His soul, that intensity of feeling and involvement. We got it in the end. Don finished the job in two weeks, and what a job it was. In February 1996, *Conflitto* was released and immediately sold twenty-five thousand copies. It completely sold out and is now regarded by many of that generation as one of the most beautiful Italian records of the 1990s.

We are still grateful to Don for devoting two weeks of his life to us. We tried to steal his secrets with our eyes. His generosity, humility, decision-making, and problem-solving enabled us to bring order to the chaos in which we found ourselves. Every detail of those days served as a teaching tool for our future artistic endeavors.

Emilio Prosperi

Assalti Frontali - Brutopop

I met Don when he came to Rome in 1995 to record *Conflitto*, in a recording studio under construction. You could tell straightaway he was a genius, and an artisan of the job. When we finished, he said: "If you want to work together again, you'll have to come to Inner Ear."

Three years later, we were flying to Washington. It was Brutopop and me, as their live sound engineer; even if we didn't have any concert planned, I couldn't have missed that train (a plane in this case). When we got there, three of us stayed

Recording session for *Conflitto*, Assalti Frontali featuring Brutopop. H.C. Musica Forte recording studio, Forte Prenestino, Rome, Italy, 1995. LEFT: (left to right) Franchino, Giannunzio Trovato, PolG, Massimino, Silvio Grillandi, Emilio Prosperi, Fabio Chinca, Don, and Luca Mascini. Photo courtesy of with Joe Lally of Fugazi and Antonia, our friend from Rome and a great photographer. Fabio and I were staying in Don's basement, once used as a recording studio, where he taped the first Bad Brains record. I remember Don telling us that when he had to record the vocals, he asked HR to go sing in the garden 'cause he was too loud and a bit too active, so I imagined all the neighbors looking at this guy screaming his lungs out and jumping around with no music.

I remember walking into Inner Ear with the feeling of entering a temple, and in a couple of days it became home. We drank liters of coffee daily, and we ate tons of bread dipped in homemade EVO that we'd brought from Italy for Don. Usually we would walk from Don's house to the studio; we wouldn't take the car because we were one too many people. Actually, when we took the car the first day, we were stopped by the police and a cop started talking on the loudspeaker. I don't remember what he told us, but it sounded pretty intimidating.

When we left the house one day it started raining; about three minutes later it was pouring. We could have gone back and taken the car or called a cab, or we could have waited out the rain, but Don wouldn't stop, not even slow down for that matter (with those long legs), so we got to the studio completely soaked. I laugh now, when I think about it, but when we got there I was furious. I slammed my jacket on the floor and hissed, "It is not funny." Dead silence. Then Don made us dry our clothes in the dryer (an unusual appliance for us at the time) and we made peace, drinking coffee and dipping bread in olive oil.

Inner Ear was a springboard for me, a turning point. I didn't go back to Rome when we finished, like the others, but took a bus to New York. I remember Don driving me to the bus station and telling me: "When I met you in Rome, I knew you were a bit of a nomad." I spent the next ten years in New York and then started to move again—I guess Don was right.

Fabio Chinca

Brutopop

Don is a tall man with a vision, a simple person, pure and sensitive.

One magical day in 1997, he invited our band to make a record at his studio. Brutopop's trip to Mecca! It was a long flight from Rome (for some of us, our first flight ever). I can't explain how good it felt to be recognized by Don as something worth his time. He came to pick us up with his car, probably a white Honda.

"Hey, guys, Fugazi just finished mixing their new one, wanna hear it?"

That's how we got to hear *End Hits* before most other people on the planet.

Music sounds totally different depending on where you listen to it, right? Looking out the window from the backseat, it sounded indigenous and so beautiful to me. We were next! How weird was that?

Some of us were kindly hosted by Joe and Antonia. Emilio and I slept at Don and Juanita's, in their basement. Right in the same room where the first Bad Brains songs were recorded . . .

Don walked his dog Cricket every morning before going to the studio. Then he walked us. A twenty-minute promenade through Arlington down to heaven. Inner Ear was the greatest place on earth, an extension of Don's personality. A wooden machine, a handmade starship, a shelter full of toys, memories, and good vibes.

It took me some time to realize such a place was opening doors for us. It was too much, really. I remember, as we were still trying to put our songs back together, Don's voice in my headphones going, "That was good! Let's move to the next one." I wish we'd had the guts to trust him more.

We wanted to give our best—we sure tried. Don's dedication made the process smooth like butter, enhancing our potential to the fullest. I consider it the peak of our musical experience.

There is still so much more to say . . . My man Brendan loaned me his drums! Ian and Adam Yauch drove us back from a Lee Perry show in DC!

Let me just add that being part of Inner Ear's legacy is a great honor. Thank you, Don.

Silvio Grillandi
Brutopop

We landed in Washington in the cold fall of 1997 to record Brutopop's *La teoria del frigo vuoto* (*Empty Fridge Theory*) in the mythical Inner Ear Studio.

I can still recall Don and Juanita's fish soup that managed to instantly erase our jet lag, and our first car ride to the studio listening to Fugazi's *End Hits*, fearing our music might not rise to the occasion.

Once we stepped into the studio, that feeling disappeared. We immediately felt at home. As soon as we opened the door, the studio welcomed us into a little living room with a TV and a small kitchen, then a long corridor leading to control rooms B and A, and finally to the beautiful, cozy recording room, full of drawings and paintings, sculptures and puppets, where lots of little light bulbs gave off a relaxing glow. Everywhere, hanging on the walls, hundreds of album covers of the recordings made there (many of which we loved through the years).

Our songs, shaky up until then, took on a new light and every tile magically found its place in the mosaic, thanks to the man behind the mixing desk, who knew how to handle, like a true coach, our tendency toward an improvisational sonic anarchy.

Three takes for each song straight to tape, some overdubs, and in three or four days all the material was recorded, ready to be mixed. But those are just technical matters, now blurring in our memory after so many years . . .

What remains is the enchantment of that place, making us feel right at home being six thousand kilometers away from our actual homes, and Don's unbelievable humanity, so sweet and funny, his humble yet solid expertise and technical creativity.

For all of us he was a true maestro, a wizard in his laboratory!

Giannunzio Trovato

Brutopop

The right things smell good, and the Inner Ear scent was so good that it has stayed in my nose for more than twenty-five years. Once in the studio, all your senses turned on. Good music, the smell of wood, coffee with vanilla, warm bread with olive oil, a clean carpet, and the most generous and kind person we had ever met in our band experiences. We entered the studio like believers into a temple, and we could feel right away that it wasn't just the music but the relationship.

Don didn't like infinite overdubs and pushed us to play the first take as well as possible, because for him, feeling counted more than precision and technique. We probably weren't truly ready to grab the best opportunity we'd ever had, but the lesson was fundamental and not only about recording. Don was the older brother everyone needed. One day he took us to the studio in his car, the small one—we were like anchovies in a can—and the next day we walked for miles in the rain, maybe to toughen us up (this is the romantic Hollywood version).

Scott Stuckey

Filmmaker

In the fall of 1997, Vic Chesnutt and I had one mission: to go to DC and record at Don Zientara's Inner Ear. We had amassed a collection of everything from rap songs to a cover of Olivia Newton John's "Have You Never Been Mellow" and wanted to archive it. We had been in Atlanta at Bobby Brown's Bosstown Studios. They had the fanciest equipment, hot-shot engineers, and all the blinking lights you could want, but nothing sounded right. It was sterile and plain. For this project we needed a more relaxed atmosphere and we knew that meant Inner Ear. And if we were going to be in DC, why not invite the guys from Fugazi? So Ian, Joe, and Brendan came by. The first song on deck was the cover of Olivia Newton John, an artist not normally associated with Fugazi or Vic. When we got there Vic said, "I'm glad we came to Don," and I knew that he was right. During the session, he and I rarely disagreed, and when we did it was normally about one thing: tempo. This song was no different. Originally, it was recorded at a poppy upbeat 122 bpm. I knew we'd be slowing it down, but not as much as Vic wanted. Don suggested a compromise using a metaphor only he understood. Vic and I were both happy. Brendan Canty still called it a funeral dirge, which was a perfect description, and it turned out wonderfully. When we finished, Vic turned to me and said, "I love Don," and I said, "I love Don too." Everyone does. Don made a recording experience more interesting than anyone. The studio was sorta like a cool new-age school, and Don was the teacher that everyone hoped to have. If music soothes the savage beast, then Don is the lion tamer. Musicians can be terribly finicky and no one handles them better than Don. That was neither our first nor our last trip to Inner Ear, but definitely one of my most memorable. We almost didn't take a photo, but after we finished, we thought we should document it. So we ran back and Vic's wife Tina snapped this moment in time.

Andy Myers

My Life in Rain

Marinara sauce, good olives, crusty bread, and red wine: this is what comes to mind when I remember Inner Ear. Oh sure, we recorded a few records, but who cares about that?

TOP: session for one song for Scott Stuckey's short film, not released, 1997. (Left to right) Vic Chesnutt (front), Joe Lally, Don Zientara, Brendan Canty, Ian MacKaye, and Scott Stuckey. BOTTOM: recording the song "Vowel Movements" for *Pancake Mountain*, 2003. Amy Farina (left) and Ian MacKaye. Photos courtesy of Scott Stuckey.

The first time I walked into Inner Ear, my bandmates and I were trying to keep our shit together as we passed a wall of album covers that made us want to start a band in the first place. Hauling gear into the main room, setting up guitars and drums, we acted like this was all normal and not some big deal. Don was genial, efficient, and tall. Like *really* tall (and I'm six four). He worked his room, set his mics, and unspooled cables like some cross between Ichabod Crane and Mikhail Baryshnikov. I don't recall sound checking, I barely remember recording, but what I remember clearly are the between times.

Our bass player was a great Italian cook and he'd bring pasta sauces, capocollo, bread, olives, and wine every day, and Don would just light up. We would break bread with him during lulls or just because we were happy making a record with Don. His delight with a simple repast and easy banter put us all at ease and relaxed us into the space needed to make records with your friends. We knew that Don knew which mic to use for a kick drum and exactly where to put it, and that our records would sound professional and good, but we didn't know that the simple act of joining us over those humble feasts would be what we would all still talk about whenever Don or Inner Ear gets mentioned some twenty-five years later.

I look forward to cooking for him someday soon.

Chris Richards

Q and Not U

I first knew Don Zientara as a name that legitimized any record it appeared on, and then as a voice that occasionally appeared in songs on those records. "'Suck My Left One,' take one, it's rolling," Don says while recording Bikini Kill at Inner Ear, quietly giving the green light for pandemonium to commence. "Okay, the following is for reference only," he says at the outset of Fugazi's *Instrument*, sounding like the punk version of Don LaFontaine, the famous movie trailer narrator. (His voice wasn't dramatic like LaFontaine's, but it had a similar air of omniscience.)

So of course my most vivid memories of working with Don involve the sound of his voice traveling from the control room to my headphones while recording the first Q and Not U album at Inner Ear in the summer of 2000. I was tracking my vocals, sounding nervous and tentative at best, when Ian MacKaye, who was producing, had an inspired suggestion: "Put on your guitar!" The idea was that feeling the weight of the instrument hanging on my shoulder might connect my body to the memory of performing live—an energy that we were now trying to capture on tape. Presto. It totally worked.

So then Don got to work, paying great attention to every syllable that came out of my twenty-one-year-old airways, gently and patiently asking me to rerun certain lines until we got everything right. Hearing myself sing had felt terrifying moments earlier, but now we were in this whole new focus-zone together. Listening to the calm in Don's voice helped me surface the energy in mine.

Throughout the session, Don and Ian were an incredible team with an almost telepathic division of labor. Ian would start each day by riling us up—playing us Fela Kuti (first time I heard him), or DJ Jubilee (same), or showing us his VHS copy of Bad Brains detonating inside CBGB circa 1982—so that we'd practically run to our instruments, eager to get to work. From there, Don would direct psychic traffic behind the mixing board, listening close and keeping the temperature down

Q and Not U

Q and Not U, *Hot and Informed* session, 1999. TOP LEFT: Chris Richards. TOP RIGHT: Harris Klahr. BOTTOM LEFT: (left to right) Don Zientara, Harris Klahr, Ian MacKaye, and Matt Borlik. BOTTOM RIGHT: mixing session for *Power*, 2004. Rafael Cohen (left) and Harris Klahr. Photos courtesy of Q and Not U.

whenever it was time to make hard decisions. It felt so thrilling and humbling all at once. These were our heroes and they were making us feel so deeply cared for.

To me, care and calm are the two inextricable tenets of Don's legacy. He knew that brash young punks could often be very fragile people, and that their brash sides could only come out if their fragile sides felt safe. Hardcore as we know it would not sound as fantastically volatile without Don's abiding serenity at the controls.

And yes, we found a way to smuggle Don's voice onto our album. You can hear him at the beginning of the song "Nine Things Everybody Knows," the word "nine" echoing through a hall-of-mirrors delay before the band kicks in. It's a relatively tiny sound-gesture, but I remember feeling like we were sneaking into our pantheon, hoping Don's voice might act like some kind of sonic watermark, putting us in the company of the bands we idolized. I hear it differently now, of course. The sound of Don's voice reminds me of how composure, empathy, and generosity can generate creativity, vitality, and intensity. It's a beautiful sound. I'm so glad it's in our music.

Peter Bauer

The Recoys - The Walkmen

The first time I recorded at Inner Ear was when I was eighteen or nineteen with my band the Recoys. All of us in the band were sort of precious and stupid in the way a nineteen-year-old might be. I think it was my first time in a proper recording studio. Don was wonderful, humoring us and guiding us through the process. He had an incredible "can do" attitude that really stuck with me. One night, we were leaving and realized our car had been blocked in by some of the neighbors in the alley. I was pretty stressed that we were stuck for the night. All four of us in the band had no idea what to do. Don came out and said very casually, "Why don't we just move the car?" We all thought this was ridiculous but we each grabbed an end and just picked up the neighbor's car and carried it out of the way. I pulled out my car and then we put the other car back. I'm pretty sure Don did most of it himself.

Ryan Nelson

Routineers - The Most Secret Method

To meet Don is to love Don. All it takes is an introduction and you'll see exactly what I mean. With that being said, I can't remember the first time I actually met him. It was probably while working at Dischord, and I was probably painfully shy and fascinated and starstruck after finally putting a face to the name on the back of every record I worshipped as a teenager.

I do, however, remember the first time I worked with him . . .

When I was in the Most Secret Method, we tried to do as much as humanly possible on our own for our first release (a two-song 7"), so we made the recording in our practice space, using my Tascam four-track cassette recorder, a pile of borrowed mics, and a compressor that I had no idea how to use. After mixing, something just didn't sound right. The bass was too subby (is that a tech term?), and we just didn't feel good about the songs. They needed help, but we didn't know

5-27-98 Tucson-

Fabulous Las Vegas by day - Unique structures and shapes against the desert horizon.

The COLLECTOR Series

Don- we were offered a weekly gig at Caeser's palace but turned it down. they wanted us to open for Dom DeLouise. But he certainly should open for us. oh well. coming home.
M/

HEY DON, WE'RE PLAYING THE HOTTEST TOWNS ON EARTH. I DON'T KNOW HOW THESE PEOPLE LIVE OUT HERE. WE'RE MELTING! SEE YA SOON.
—RYAN.

NEW ORLEANS LA 701 1998

USA 20

Don Zientara
2701 S. Oakland
Arlington VA

©1996 RENO-TAHOE SPECIALTY, INC. 2901 S. Highland # 13A Las Vegas, Nevada 89132 Photo 42B-4-3 By: Brent Printed in Hong Kong

3-004-09000-0655

Space below reserved for U. S. POSTAL SERVICE

what kind of help. So we called Don. My brother and I brought the mixes to him, and Don quickly worked some magic (setting the parametric EQ), and he fixed our first release. He was pleasant and kind and accommodating, and I left feeling like I had just worked with a legend.

Later, I was fortunate to record at Inner Ear quite a bit. I recorded there with J. Robbins, Chad Clark, TJ Lipple, and, of course, Don and Ian. Looking back at all the time I spent in that studio, I have pretty serious regret in never trying to work there. I should've made some sort of an attempt at becoming an unpaid intern, a fly on the wall, learning everything I could through hands-on experience. Soaking up as much Don-time as possible.

Don's a surfer. I think once you start to see him that way, everything clicks into place. He's Zen-like and unpretentious. There's peace and humor, wit, intelligence, big smiles, and deadpan delivery all at the same time. He's a professional without an obtrusive ego. Never condescending. He's approachable and honest. He works joyfully, methodically, and doesn't bullshit around.

He's also fascinatingly strange. Like my favorite kind of strange.

Around 2006, I bought a cheap car from a friend and immediately drove it to work at Dischord. Don was the first person I saw when I pulled up, and I excitedly told him, "Hey, check out this car I just bought for five hundred bucks!"

He seemed genuinely excited for me and then said a peculiar thing: "Alright! Well, let's open it up and have a look."

"Um . . . you mean open the hood?"

"Yeah, open it up." He was already at the front of my car. I opened the hood and the two of us peered at the innards of this 1991 Corolla, and Don said, "Yep, it's all there," and shut the hood.

I wish I had a thimbleful of Don's charm and knowledge. He's been wildly influential to me . . . not just because of the records he's engineered, and not just because he's kind and welcoming to everyone, and not because he fixed my eight-track for free when I was broke, and not because there isn't another human on earth who can shamelessly enter a room rockin' just a pair of shorts and flip-flops quite like he can. Don's been a friend and mentor to me. His personality and work ethic is something to aspire to. I love him.

Sit next to him sometime. You'll see what I mean.

Hugh McElroy

Black Eyes

Recorded at Inner Ear Studio was printed in the liner notes of a ridiculous number of records in my suburban-DC-teenage-punk collection. *Black Dots*, early Bad Brains recordings Don made, propelled me, more than anything else, into taking recording seriously as something I wanted to do (and prompted some pivotal gear purchases).

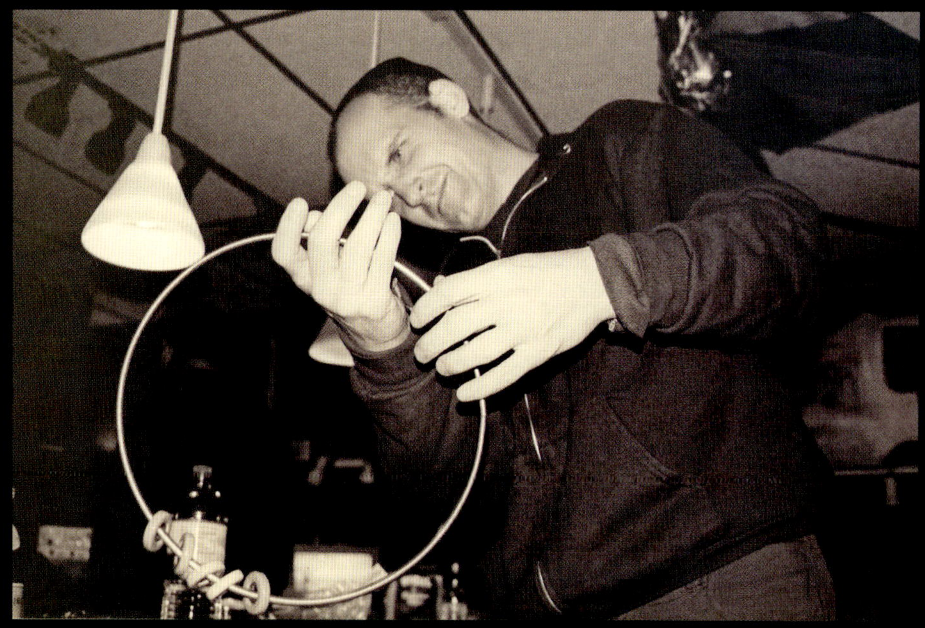

Black Eyes *S/T* session, 2002. LEFT: Daniel Martin-McCormick (left) and Hugh McElroy. RIGHT: Ian MacKaye trying to figure out how to solve the game. Photos by Dan Caldas.

I ultimately had the pleasure of working on records at Inner Ear as a musician, an engineer, an assistant engineer, and an assistant producer, on and off between 2001 and 2016. Working in that studio, it's hard not to feel Part Of Something. The albums on the walls, the signatures in the repair room, the DC punk family tree in the hallway—it never got old or lost its shine.

The gear is cool. The artifacts are cool. The tape room is very cool. But here's a list of the even cooler things about my work there:

- The insane number of books and puzzles in the control room.

- Don showing up with fresh bread and putting it out with a little dish of olive oil, salt, and red pepper flakes.

- Don setting me up to record there for the first time, putting me to work soldering connectors onto an eight-channel TRS snake and just letting me figure it out despite not having soldered anything in fifteen years.

- Don letting me know without anger or reproach that I was using some gear pretty recklessly.

- Having dinner at Don and Juanita's, cooked by the Japanese band Shift, who were staying with them while he recorded them (and finding out Don had cut his teeth on the same Shure microphone mixer I had).

- Don's profound gift for creating a space in which hard work—making records is often laborious and repetitive—is often as joyful in the moments of difficulty as in the moments of triumph.

Rafael Cohen

El Guapo - !!!

El Guapo recorded at Inner Ear twice in the back room, once with J. Robbins and once with Chad Clark. We also mixed a record there with Chad but we never worked with Don.

That said, I did want to speak about my time mixing the Q and Not U album *Power* at Inner Ear. Q and Not U were very close friends of mine and a far more successful band than El Guapo ever was. After making two records with Ian and Don, they decided they wanted to work with me and Pete from my band on their third album, *Power*, in 2003. We recorded the record in New York but went down to Inner Ear to mix it. This was my first experience ever "producing" or mixing a record on my own for another band. And I felt a lot of pressure since Q was a popular act and they had a beloved discography. Even though we were young and enthusiastic we were also inexperienced and fairly inept at the technical aspects of using the studio.

Don was absolutely amazing the entire time. He never condescended to us in any way; he sat patiently as we tried to figure things out . . . offered a helping hand if he thought he could . . . and answered every question no matter how basic. I remember thinking that rather than feeling in any way territorial about this band that he had made amazing records with, he just tried to help us get the sound we wanted for that project. I was so grateful for his patience, his kindness, and his advice throughout that whole process. Don helped you make the record you wanted to make. It's such a simple, easy, and direct sentiment . . . and one that is so rare in the recording industry. He helped you get to where you wanted to go. Really . . . what better thing could be said about a recording engineer?

Steve Dore

Deep Lust - Casual Dots

Recording at Inner Ear was as pleasurable as can be. I immediately felt at ease with Don's warmth and particularly dry sense of humor. He also has plenty of patience, which is incredibly important in any creative environment. Inner Ear always seemed like such an apt name for the studio as he really provides a free and open environment for people to record sounds the way they see fit, and the proof is in the wide-eyed and wild recordings he has been involved in.

Alirio González

Machetres

I believe the first time we met Don was in December of 2003 when we were coming in to record our full-length record at Inner Ear. We had spoken over the phone a few times to set it up but had never actually met. We rang the bell and Don answered the door. The first thing I thought was, *How is he not cold?* because he was wearing shorts, sandals, and a T-shirt in like thirty-degree weather. He greeted and welcomed us and gave us a quick tour of the place. The studio experience in general can be a bit intimidating, at least for me, especially when you know about all the amazing artists that have recorded at Inner Ear throughout the years. I'm also not much of a gear head and I probably couldn't tell you what many of those racks and knobs in the studio do, but I didn't need to because Don knew and he was more than happy to share his knowledge. I remember him asking for all the lyrics to our songs, and since many of them were in Spanish, he asked me to translate them so he could get a sense and feeling of the song. At one point my guitar started buzzing like crazy, so he quickly cracked it open and soldered some wires, and in no time we were ready to go. There were replacement guitars but both he and I knew that the sound I wanted was from that particular one. He really cared and respected our time there and that feeling was reciprocal. We recorded twelve songs in three days, the three of us in one room playing live, with the exception of some overdubs and vocals, and we had a blast doing it. What I've come to realize over the years of recording in different places is that you can really feel the connection with Don and Inner Ear. It was like his second home and he invited you in and made you feel like it was your home too.

The last time I saw him was during our final recording session at Inner Ear. I believe it was at the end of 2012. This time we were there for three days but only did three songs, which would become our 7" *Sopa de Res*. On the final day of the session, right after we were done mixing the last song, he looked up at us from his chair by the console and said something like, "You guys like chili? I got a friend who has a chili spot nearby. My treat." To which we replied, "Hell yeah!!!" So we jumped in my tiny car which was completely crashed on one side. I apologized for the condition of the car and the door not opening all the way, and he said something like, "You don't need to apologize, it's just a means of transportation to take us from point A to point B," and we drove to eat chili. It made me view the studio that way—not as a wrecked car but as a vessel, a means of transportation, a spaceship to take you from point A to point B. From the ideas in your head and heart to a record in your hand.

Machetres

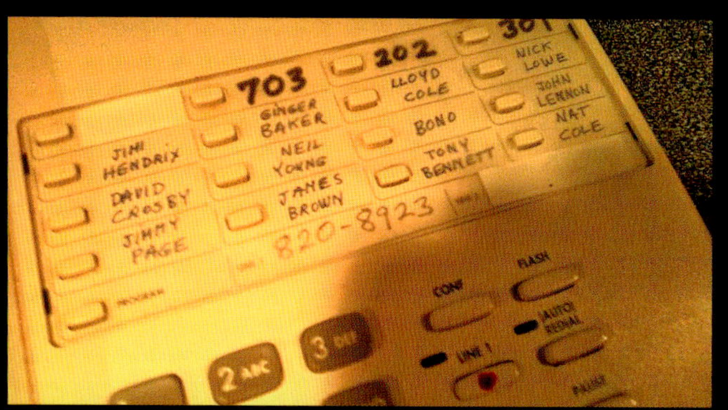

Machetres *S/T* session, 2003. TOP LEFT: Alirio González (left) and Don. Photo by Cristian Gajardo. TOP RIGHT: *S/T* CD sleeves, 2003. (Left to right) Paul González, Alirio González, and Cristian Gajardo. Photo by Lilo González Sr. MIDDLE LEFT: 7" session, 2012. Cristian Gajardo. Photo by Lilo González Jr. MIDDLE RIGHT: 7" session, 2012. Alirio González. Photo by Cristian Gajardo. BOTTOM: Telephone with some VIP numbers, 2012. Photo by Cristian Gajardo.

Let me point out that it was winter and Don hopped in the car wearing his signature shorts, sandals, and T-shirt. I think he might have been wearing a light outdoor vest this time. I just think Don has warmth to spare.

Next time we see him, we are definitely taking him out for chili. Our treat!!

Jerry Busher

John Frusciante (*DC EP*) - Fugazi - French Toast - All Scars

John and I met when he came to some Fugazi shows in 2001. It was a thrill, I am a longtime fan of his guitar playing and boundless creativity. I was on drums, percussion, and trumpet, and it was exciting to get his feedback on my playing.

We started talking about collaborating while on a tour my band French Toast did with the Red Hot Chili Peppers in 2003. He told me about his six-albums-in-six-months project and that he was reserving four songs for the session with me. John and I spoke about it being a stripped-down recording that supported the song first and foremost. He sent me demos recorded in a hotel room with an acoustic guitar. I talked about wanting to play brushes, which I did on the song "Repeating," my personal favorite.

John asked Ian to produce and we booked two days at Inner Ear with Don. Ian attended a rehearsal the day before at my studio in DC. He was very involved in the direction of the recording. I love to collaborate and this was a great experience all around.

We got to Inner Ear the next day and started tracking the drums and guitar live in the room face-to-face! It was intense to record songs live-to-tape on one rehearsal with one of my favorite musicians! Having Ian and Don there was a great comfort. Inner Ear feels like home and the atmosphere helped me feel comfortable and just play.

We did a few takes and immediately went on to record John on bass, vocals, and second guitar, all tracked with us sitting together in the control room. I added some percussion and we moved on to mixing. Four songs recorded and mixed in two days.

I am very proud of this record and cherish that day with John and everyone.

John Frusciante

Red Hot Chili Peppers - Ataxia

In 1998, Fugazi was my favorite current rock band, and as fate would have it, I started to become friendly with them. Over the ensuing years, Ian and I had some interesting conversations about the correlation between record and budget. The first time I made a solo record in a professional studio was in 2002. The record was very difficult to make. I was so determined to make it "perfect" that it took almost four months and cost $150,000. In contrast, Ian's philosophy was that economy should be integral to art. Fugazi had never spent more than $10,000 on a record, usually completing them within a month. Their aim was to capture a feeling that was real, as opposed to trying to fight human imperfection.

That the art of recording and economic considerations could work in harmony with one another, rather than being at odds, had become an inspiring idea for me. In 2003, I had a six-month break from my band, and decided I would make six records in those six months. The plan was to record and mix each record within a two-week period, and spend around $10,000 per record, and that is more or less what I managed to do.

A couple of months into this process, Ian invited me to come stay at his house and make a record at Inner Ear with Don Zientara. I was a great admirer of Don, particularly all the Dischord stuff he had recorded. I was trying to do in LA what I believed those guys had generally been doing in DC, in terms of embracing so-called flaws, moving fast, and keeping it econo, so the thought of actually recording at Inner Ear was very exciting. So many of my favorite records had been recorded there.

I showed up with no guitar. The plan was to record and mix an EP of four songs in two days, and that is exactly what we did. Jerry Busher was to play the drums, and we had one rehearsal the day before recording. He instinctively knew just what to play.

Don's energy was very calming. He struck me as being somewhat shy and mild mannered, yet a stabilizing, grounding presence. Ian wound up producing the session. He kept the communication happening and kept things rolling along. He was a great idea man as well, especially concerning what *not* to do, and he saved me from myself in a few places. He and

John Frusciante recording session, 2004. (Back) Don, (front, left to right) John Frusciante, Jerry Busher, and Ian MacKaye. Photo by G.L. Jaguar.

Don had a great rapport, which made me feel good about just playing and leaving the details of recording in their hands. Jerry and I performed the basic tracks effortlessly, as if we had been recording together for years.

I played the basic rhythm guitar tracks on Ian's SG through Fugazi's Marshall amp. For lead guitar overdubs I played Guy Picciotto's Les Paul Junior, and used the bass that was there in the studio. At Ian and Don's suggestion, the vocals were sung without headphones, listening instead through the control room speakers, a first for me.

I was focused on looking forward to imperfections of performance, rather than recording in fear of them. It was a great atmosphere for that mindset, because there was a good feeling between the four of us, so there was nothing to hide. I spent quite a bit of time laughing, as those guys' sense of humor was ever-present, and as effortless for them as breathing.

Don had a very gentle approach, and everything he did was perfect. He did not assert himself on the music, but rather had the sensitivity to respond to the vibe of the songs. I wanted everything to sound very intimate, with minimal compression and no reverb, and Don was comfortable with that. More importantly, he knew how to make those restrictions sound good.

In this case, we did a very soft, understated record, but it makes sense to me that people have gone so wild with Don at the desk. His anchored, mellow vibe gives you a foundation to feel free. For me, that meant keeping the flow going, so we could capture performances that I was happy with in one or two takes. The idea was to record these soft songs punk rock style, and the selfless commitment of all those present made it sound like what it was.

It's an experience I'll always be grateful for, one of those times in life that becomes even more meaningful as time goes by.

Angela Melkisethian

Crucial Defect - Hott Beat - Partyline

It was always enjoyable and easygoing at Inner Ear. It was the ultimate recording safety zone. Partyline recorded our album there; my bands Crucial Defect and Hott Beat both mixed there.

Most of the bands I was in had a recording budget of two hundred dollars or so. To make the most of our modest funds we would record in bedrooms, cheaper studios, and the like, and then go to Inner Ear for mixing to "fix" our recordings, which Don of course did!

It was great to finally fully record and mix there with Partyline and producer Chris Richards—I have fond memories especially of recording the group vocals, standing around a single mic girl-group style. That was probably the most fun I've had recording anything!

For Hott Beat, I recall my bandmate bringing a boom box with something or other on cassette—playing this for Don as an example of how we envisioned our album's sound. He took it in stride!

Justin Duerr

Northern Liberties

I truly feel like one of Don Zientara's gifts as a person—beyond his skill as a studio engineer—is that he exudes patience and brings a great ability to listen. I get the feeling he's the type who can transcend his own "taste" in music, for example, to get into the space where he's thinking, *This may not be my cup of tea, but what is it that people who like it see in it? How can I succeed in documenting it accurately within that framework?* Very non-ego based. I think that's just such a perfect attitude for a recording engineer to have. So I felt very calm and focused while recording with him—which also makes for a better performance and use of time! I felt like recording at Inner Ear was more like, *Wow, we have this giant box of tools here, let's dive in and see what we can do!* There was a true creative synergy, which is just as important as having all the high-end mics, etc.

Aaron Leitko

SPRCSS

In 2010, I was playing bass in SPRCSS. I was the rookie in the group. It was Bob and Daneil's band, really, though recently augmented with Justin Moyer, who had invited me aboard. We booked a single day at Inner Ear to record with Ian and Don.

The afternoon prior, the four of us gathered at Justin's place in DC to rehearse. That part didn't go so hot. There was an argument and somebody threatened to bail. Ian popped by to check in and was able to smooth things over, but raw feelings remained.

Once we loaded into the studio, though, that tension mostly vanished. This was one of Inner Ear's greatest assets: it was easy to get comfortable. It was a professional recording studio that somehow retained the lived-in coziness of a suburban basement—complete with random junk and ponderous ephemera.

I loved the kitchen area in particular, where LP jackets from local bands were stuck hither and thither on the wall. There was no discernible order to their arrangement and thus no implied hierarchy. This seemed to suggest alignment and harmony across the myriad styles, cliques, and time lines of DC music. The decor encouraged creativity and defused ego.

Ian and Don set us up right in front of the control room, guiding everybody into a compact space that mirrored the tight confines of our practice arrangement. This was a good call. What we gave up in isolation, we got back in confidence. SPRCSS songs were exciting to play. It felt necessary to watch one another and to feel the volume and energy of the music physically. On at least one track, I can hear us start loose and glue together as the music gains in velocity. This is technically a "mistake," but it captures something essential about my experience of the band.

I'll miss Inner Ear. Going there—to record, to hang out, to learn to degauss tape heads—always felt like a relief, almost like going home for the holidays. You were on safe ground and in good hands.

Northern Liberties

Northern Liberties *Ghost Mind Electricity* session, 2007. TOP LEFT: outside Inner Ear. (Left to right) Kevin Riley, Marc Duerr, and Justin Duerr. TOP RIGHT: (left to right) Don, Justin Duerr, and Marc Duerr. BOTTOM LEFT: Justin Duerr. BOTTOM RIGHT: Don (left) and Justin Duerr. Photos by Kevin Riley.

Lise Bruneau

Taffety Punk Theatre Company

Walking into the historic and humble sanctum of Inner Ear, where many of my most precious punk, rock, and alternative records were made, it was impossible to avoid feeling as if maybe this wasn't the place to lay down a track of the marvelous poem "The Rape of Lucrece." Certainly the man who engineered *Steady Diet of Nothing* would have little interest in a long narrative poem by William Shakespeare. As soon as I shook Don's hand, all of those fears were set at bay. He was so excited about embarking on new territory. He had so many questions about what we wanted the piece to feel like to the listener, and was so utterly engaged throughout the process. Clearly, Inner Ear was the perfect call.

Listening to the audio (which at this date is still a ways from its release), there is such immediacy in the tone, and such richness—but like with Fugazi and all who were fortunate to work with him, it feels like the artist is in the room with you NOW: the work is happening right in front of you. You have a front-row seat for the event.

Our theatre company, Taffety Punk, was born from and celebrates our punk roots. I think it is always a little pleasantly surprising how gracefully our theatrical aesthetic goes hand in glove with the mechanisms of good old DC punk; and the verve and challenge and high-minded grit of commitment is part of every bastion of DC punk's history and present.

Yeah, I walked around the drum kits in the studio and imagined the delicious din that was the more usual fare from Inner Ear, but Don's craft and passion for the SOUND of the thing was able to reach into the sweet nuances of Shakespeare's language as well, and help create a unique piece that we will always be so proud (and way humbled) that he had a hand in creating.

Taffety Punk session for "The Rape of Lucrece," 2021. Lise Bruneau (left) and Don. Photo by Marcus Kyd.

Marcus Kyd

Taffety Punk Theatre Company - The Most Secret Method

Over the years, as I learned what was possible in the studio, I learned to prepare as much as possible before going in to record. That includes trying stuff out at home, like guitar and vocal overdubs, or wild mixing ideas. It saves time. And if you come in with ideas, the recording studio is a great place to collaborate, particularly with a superb engineer like Don, or J., or Chad. Their expertise at what they do makes their input invaluable.

I often tell people who are new to it to trust the person making the recording. You don't need to know what every dial and switch does. I remember when the Most Secret Method was recording with J., we could say something like, "I want this bit to sound like it is underwater," and he would figure out how to do that. Or sometimes the sound you want eludes your ability to describe it, then the engineer can get really creative.

With Taffety Punk, we have gone in to make recordings for very specific production needs. It is wonderful when the engineer has a chance to respond to those goals—be it something experimental like creating a haunting melody that should sound like it is bleeding through walls, or something more clean like the audiobook we just recorded with Don. Everyone in the room takes on the needs of the project and nurtures it. That's always been my experience at Inner Ear.

Obviously, I love it.

Justin Moyer

El Guapo - SPRCSS - E.D. Sedgwick - Light Beams

Don emails me compliments about little stories I write for a newspaper. One story was about a fox that bit a congressman. Someone said the fox was protecting her kits. Kits are baby foxes. The congressman had to get rabies shots and the fox was euthanized. Don sees stories like these and takes the time to say he appreciated them. So that means Don either 1) actually finds these stories interesting, or 2) doesn't find them interesting but is nice. Whichever is true, I think Don's emails show that he is a class act. He makes me feel good after spending hours writing a few hundred words about a possibly rabid dead fox as democracy in America collapses.

Once, in this new century's first decade, I read an ad in the print newspaper for a sixteen-track, one-inch tape machine for sale deep in the Virginia wilds. Price: $1,000. I knew next to nothing about tape machines and got ten hundred-dollar bills out of the bank and asked Don to take a ride to check it out with me. To my surprise, he agreed. He's just the kind of guy who likes taking long rides to see random tape machines.

We got to the house where the tape machine was. This fellow had built a somewhat elaborate studio in his exurban home. I was suspicious. Was this a lemon—or a reasonably priced, functioning analog machine listed for sale in the analog paper because its owner couldn't figure out Craigslist? And was the guy into country or rock and roll? I think the guy had one of those mirrors that's also a whiskey advertisement. You see why I was confused.

Don took the tape machine through the paces. It appeared to work. I gave the guy the hundred-dollar bills and Don

Don at the mixing board, 2021. Photo by Jerry Martineau.

helped load the machine into my Toyota Matrix even though the Matrix wasn't made to hold tape machines. We sort of shoved the machine in there on its side. Don was good at shoving because he is very tall and strong. Then a few years went by and the tape machine sat around while two houses I lived in were renovated. The tape machine's vinyl cover was supposed to protect it, but there was a lot of dust and I can't deny that the machine got jostled by folks who should have known better.

Finally, I got the tape machine in a place where it could be used, but I found it didn't work anymore. Don came over to look at it and he fixed what he could but it still didn't work perfectly, and after I spent another thousand dollars, I realized it wasn't worth fixing. Things break and can't be fixed—this is how the new century works.

But Don tried his best. He keeps things alive. We also had a fun ride.

Eugene Hutz

Gogol Bordello

We set out to do some work at Inner Ear for a simple reason—every record we did, we thought of it as a collaboration with a sonic vortex of a very particular kind. After self-producing a few records, and after working with Steve Albini, Jim Sclavunos, Victor Van Vugt, and Rick Rubin, who all had very particular approaches, the idea was to go where a lot of our favorite hardcore records came from.

I was very influenced by Fugazi, Dag Nasty, Bad Brains, Faith, Embrace, Void . . . Rites of Spring, Embrace . . . so was Oliver Charles, our drummer then. There was a deep connection on that level. I still got all these records on my wall. Plus all the transient projects like Egg Hunt all had a very particular sonic-lab vibe that we wanted to kind of join forces with.

Working with Don was exactly the vibe we were

Gogol Bordello, *Seekers and Finders* session, 2014. Eugene Hutz (left) and Don. Photo courtesy of Don Zientara.

seeking: always on the side of high energy, always championing taste . . . less is more . . . but also knowing when more is more, something a lot of people forget, and not so down with any smoke and mirrors . . . helping along to thrive for maximum potential but in very pure documentarian way. Needless to say, working with maniacs like we are needs stamina too, and what stamina Don Z. has! Because days were immediately followed by enjoyable after-hangs and listening to some Dischord nuggets . . . He really blew Oliver and me out of the water with some deep Dischord cuts. We were literally close to activating the circle pit in the control room. And when Ian came by, it was just an incredible vibe absolutely. We talked about music and adventures on this planet for hours.

In that atmosphere high on the vibe, we recorded and developed material for two Gogol albums: some are on *Seekers and Finders*, and some are only yet to come on this new album, *Solidaritine*, including a cover of Fugazi's iconic "Blueprint." Man, I'm so glad we did that with you, Don Z.! Grateful forever for the experience in the vortex of Inner Ear where so much of my favorite music came from!

Joe Gorelick

Garden Variety - Bluetip - Retisonic

My best recollection of the incredible (and tall) Don Zientara was the initial offering by my first punk trio, Garden Variety. I guess we were sort of the second wave of emo . . . though not really, more a hard-hitting, postpunk band with lots of melodies that threw us into that milieu. Of course, none of this mattered to Don. Don, to me, was simply a laid-back, nice guy in shorts, just need to push the record button and "you three be you" kind of guy. I loved his deep voice on the talkback so much that he is the first thing you ever hear on the first Garden Variety 7". "'Hedge' . . . take one . . . it's rolling . . ." is forever etched into my brain, and those who hear it, and if Garden Variety ever did a reunion show (unlikely), that recording would have to begin the special evening.

Recording in that room for three young, hungry guys from Queens and Long Island was a soak-up-vibe kind of session. We knew driving down there that this thing, this Dischord/DC/Virginia thing, was where we were at. Minneapolis was just way too far and NYC didn't really cut it, it had to be Don's place, and to this day it was the right decision. Don was nice to us and it was a very, very positive experience for all—long live the king!

We will miss his brilliance.

Mark Cisneros

Hammered Hulls

Hearing Don Zientara's voice on the other end of the headphones is a uniquely heartening experience. There's nothing else like it. Disarming like a lifelong family doctor and reassuring like a Zen master—a surfing Zen master. Like the man himself, Inner Ear is the opposite of the cold, hard-surfaced industry recording studios.

The man and his studio are warm, welcoming, and full of history, humor, and wit. I've been very fortunate to have

Hammered Hulls

Hammered Hulls session, 2021. TOP LEFT: Drum setup. Photo by Chris Wilson. TOP RIGHT: Don. Photo by Mark Cisneros. BOTTOM LEFT: Alec MacKaye. Photo by Mark Cisneros. BOTTOM RIGHT: Guitar setup. Photo by Chris Wilson.

recorded there a few times, and I very much appreciate the importance of working on two of the last records to be made there with Scream and Hammered Hulls.

It takes something very special to have kept this studio working for so many years and to have helped give the world so many iconic and classic recordings.

Don is that special thing. We celebrate this man. Thank you, Maestro!

Andy Sullivan

Airport 77s

"The Steely Dan Snare Scare"

It just wasn't happening. The Airport 77s were trying to pull together our first batch of songs, tweaking knobs and faders on Don's mixing board. The bass thumped, the cymbals shimmered, and the guitars snarled. But there was still something missing.

Don plugged a cartridge into one of his black boxes. "Let's try the Steely Dan snare," he said.

The "Steely Dan snare"?!

This was blasphemy. Inner Ear was no ordinary recording studio; it was where uncompromising underground types went to make records unpolluted by the mainstream. Obsolete technology was a crucial part of the equation: Don recorded the initial tracks to tape, like they did back in the twentieth century, and his computer hadn't been updated since Operation Desert Storm. The music captured here wasn't auto-tuned, time-shifted, or airbrushed. It was real, man.

Now, here in the temple of DC hardcore, the high priest was suggesting that we double John's snare with a prerecorded snippet of yacht rock.

Wasn't this cheating? Wouldn't we sacrifice our indie credibility? Would we next have to patch in the frilly guitar bits from "More Than a Feeling"?

"No, it's fine," Don said, "Fugazi used the Steely Dan snare all the time."

Well, if Fugazi did it, it must be okay.

This was the secret sauce of Inner Ear. Not the legendary LP covers lining the halls, not the vintage German microphones, not the paintings that brightened the dim control room. It was Don's ability to slice through punk metaphysics and interband tensions to give the music the slight nudge it needed.

We dialed in the Steely Dan snare, and the track sprang to life.

Airport 77s, *Rotation* session, 2021. TOP: (left to right) John Kelly, Andy Sullivan, and Don. BOTTOM: Inner Ear back entrance from the alley. Photos by Chuck Dolan.

Holly Eney

Poisonous H

On August 24, 2021, I walked into Inner Ear Studio. That act alone was not unique. I had walked through that door many times before. First, as an observing nonmusician, sitting in at recording sessions. Then, later on, as a photographer taking shots of the studio's interior for Don's website. This time, however, was different. Now I was carrying a bass, and going into the legendary Inner Ear with my band, Poisonous H . . . to be recorded by the equally legendary Don Zientara.

And this was happening just a few weeks before my forty-ninth birthday. My passion for music and desire to perform it has been with me my entire life. Yet up until a year ago, I had never picked up an instrument.

Our session that night was a success and felt like it was over way too soon. Although I was over the moon about what we had just created it was tinged with a hint of sadness, because I knew that within a month, Inner Ear would close its doors.

This would be my first . . . and last time recording there.

Thinking about my own Inner Ear experience as an actual musician made me wonder what has always made this studio such a special place. How could it have such unique and inspiring energy, and how could that energy exist consistently for over forty years?

And the answer to the above questions, I believe, is quite simply: Don Zientara. Proof of this is in the countless classic records that have emerged from Inner Ear and the almost unprecedented amount of repeat business the studio has enjoyed since it opened. Don's approach to people and his technical brilliance, in my experience, made recording a positive process.

The art on the walls, the collection of toys and tchotchkes in the control room, and the overall warm vibe of the space are entirely down to Don and his particular energy.

I guess the best way to describe what I feel when I think about Inner Ear is that it feels like home.

TOP LEFT: tape baking oven built by Don in 2005 using a Fugazi guitar cabinet shipping crate. RIGHT: (top to bottom) Ampex tape preamp, Focusrite 424 mic pres, ADL compressor, Orban compressor, and Aphex aural exciter. MIDDLE LEFT: inside view of the tape baking oven. BOTTOM LEFT: Tascam 22-4 tape recorder. Photos by Brendan Canty, 2021.

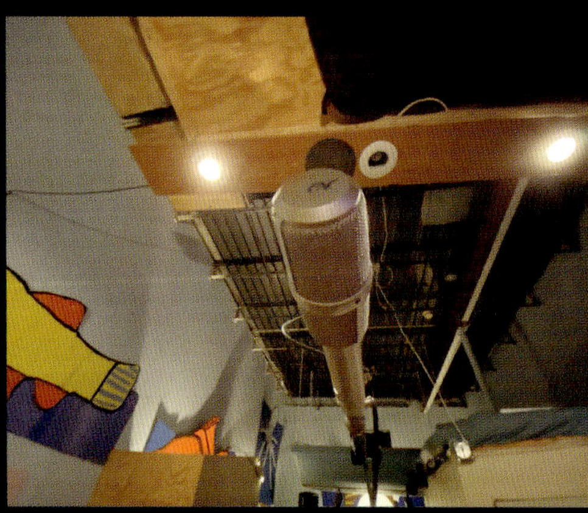

TOP LEFT: mixing desk with speakers. TOP RIGHT: cassettes. MIDDLE RIGHT: cassettes. BOTTOM LEFT: Christmas tree with brain-teaser toys. BOTTOM CENTER: Neumann SM69 stereo mic. BOTTOM RIGHT: cassettes. Photos by Brendan Canty, 2021.

TOP: Brendan Canty in the mirror taking a photo of Don. BOTTOM LEFT: Joe Lally with a brain-teaser toy. BOTTOM RIGHT: reel-to-reel boxes for archival storage of audio tapes. Photos by Brendan Canty, 2021.

Don playing a show for the Inner Ear closing party at the New District Brewery on S. Oakland Street, Arlington, 2021. Photo by Holly Eney.

Part III

Engineers and Producers

Ted Niceley
Producer

I think the first time I worked on anything at Inner Ear was when I tagged along with Skip Groff there. It was a Sunday.

He and DC's Slickee Boys were going into the studio to record what became *Forbidden Alliance*, the Slickees's breakthrough EP that contained the track "Gotta Tell Me Why." Don was engineering, of course, and that was the beginning of my relationship with him and the studio.

I came back when the guys in Fugazi asked me to work with them on the *7 Songs* EP.

I worked with Fugazi and Don engineering the *3 Songs* EP, *Repeater*, and *In on the Kill Taker*, as well. *IOTKT* was the only Fugazi record I did in the new building, when Inner Ear became twenty-four-track. I ended up working at Inner Ear a lot but with Eli Janney, who had become the house engineer. Two records with the High Back Chairs, the High Llamas, Edsel, and others.

Don is always a very cool head in the studio, patient, sort of quiet, observant, always quick to have a laugh, and most of all, kind.

I'm not sure if anyone else is thinking about this, but Don and Inner Ear have entered the realm of the iconic, and that is a great place to reside, when one moves on.

Inner Ear is as important and as much of a touchstone to many as Muscle Shoals, Motown, Stax, and Sun studios, to name the very few that represent(ed) a sound, something in particular.

Don and Inner Ear, thank you for being you.

Let's celebrate!

High Back Chairs, *Of Two Minds* session, 1990–91. TOP: Ted Niceley, BOTTOM: Eli Janney vacuuming Ted's chair. Photos by Charles Steck.

Joey Picuri

Sound Engineer

One of the coolest things about hanging out with Don Z. is the fact that if you asked him a technical question, he would invariably pull out a blank sheet of paper and draw a diagram. He may be explaining signal flow, effects patching, or getting to the best place for a burrito. I'm sure Eli Janney shared many a drawing that started on a blank piece of paper.

The first time I remember going over to Inner Ear was with Don Fleming and the Velvet Monkeys. I had never been in a studio before; I was starting to gig around DC at the Ontario Theater, 9:30 Club on F Street, DC Space, and the Bayou, where I met Don Fleming and Elaine Barnes of the Velvet Monkeys. We go around the back of a nicely kept brick house and descend into the basement where I met Don Z. and get my first look at the control room. I'm checking out this unique mixer that's totally different from anything I've worked on. I'm standing with the two very tall Dons who are both eclectic in opposite but not-unlike-each-other ways. The mixer at Inner Ear, Ivy Street, was built by Don and made sense in every way, but it was just different, and that took a bit of new thinking.

Don did a lot of things differently, but there was definitely a method to the madness, and a DIY perspective permeated most everything. PZM mics were relatively new to the industry in the '80s and Don Z. came up with his own modified version that saw the microphone element mounted on a piece of plexiglass which gave the mic the "pressure zone" it needed, but also provided some baffling, and you could still see through it, which helped keep things from feeling too cluttered. It was different, it made sense, and it worked really well, a good summation of the technical side of Doctor Z. It was also just little bit "off" and I adored that.

I started calling Don "Doctor Z" because I love the way he cuts the tape. He was so fluid and methodical, not unlike a surgeon. That was not only a testimony to his technical prowess but the musicality and artistry that really completes the package. It takes all of that to really edit tape well. I was curious to see how that editing technique translated to the digital world. During the recent Scream *DC Special* sessions, I watched Doctor Z edit a different beginning section onto a track that had already been recorded. My son Ellis and I were alone with Don in the control room as he went to work. I felt like that same kid years ago as I watched him work the magic in the digital realm. Wow—he nailed it. You would never know there were two different takes with two different drummers, and the band could get on with their work knowing they had the take they wanted.

Don Z. has a lot of special sauces by his side as he provides the musicians and artists the place to create. The quiet confidence he exudes helps everyone to reach for their best and he rarely makes a technical mistake and he is usually tactful but honest about a take or a part being played. He's the coolest engineer/producer in shorts and flip-flops and he's a great guy to hang out with. I know this firsthand as we once spent three weeks together in Sicily recording thirteen bands.

He's the fucking best.

Scream, *This Side Up* session, 1985. LEFT: (left to right) Don, Pete Stahl, and Joey Picuri. RIGHT: Joey Picuri. Photos courtesy of Joey Picuri.

Eli Janney

Sound Engineer and Producer / Girls Against Boys

I first met Don back in 1984. I was just getting interested in recording music, and knew nothing. My older brother Eddie was in a band, and I had gone along with them to see Inner Ear Studio and watch them record. Don was very patient answering all my idiot questions, explaining not just how to do things but also why they worked. For those who have never met Don, he is exceedingly calm and Zen, a great disposition for teaching and for making records.

Two years later, as a college student, I tried to get an internship at Inner Ear for my radio and TV program at George Washington University. Don was into the idea (the studio was getting very busy at the time) but unfortunately GW didn't have a music production course they could give me credit for, so the school turned it down. When I called Don to tell him the bad news, he just said: "Okay, why don't you just work here?" And just like that, the course of my life changed. I spent the next five years working with Don and learning how to record and mix bands; he taught me pretty much everything there is to know about audio engineering. It was an amazing time in my life, the first time I ever got so into something that I lost track of time.

Two things happened during that time that stick with me. After I had been working there maybe six months, with barely a grasp of how to engineer, there was an unexpected death in Don's family. We had been booking the studio with two engineers, so it was a full schedule day and night. Don had to leave town and said, "You take these sessions." I was pretty stunned—I barely knew what I was doing. But Don believed in me and so I just did it. I was forced to really figure out quickly how to record anything and everything, plus deal with all types of personalities and work two shifts a day. It made me a much better engineer.

The other was when I met Ted Niceley. Don had it in his mind that Ted and I would work well together; I have no idea why he thought this but he did. Ted liked working with Don and didn't want to try anybody new. So on the next session with Ted, Don had me come in to "assist." As the session started, he said, "I have to go to the store," and left me to run the session while he was gone. And then he just didn't return! Ted kept asking, "When is Don coming back?" and I truly had no idea. Of course, by the end of the day we were having a great time and getting some seriously good work done. I ended up engineering for Ted for the next few years all over the world, including some amazing sessions in France and the UK, all thanks to Don. Don was as close to a mentor as I've ever had in my life; he truly changed the course of my life and showed me how to encourage creativity in all my sessions.

Geoff Turner

Sound Engineer and Producer / Gray Matter - 3

There is an important group of individuals who built the creative spaces in the Washington area that collected, focused, and amplified the nascent 1980s underground music scene. I'm thinking of people like Susan and Bill Warrell (DC Space), Bobby Ferrando (Food for Thought restaurant), Skip Groff (Yesterday and Today Records), and Don Zientara of Inner Ear Studio.

Don Z. appeared to all of us punk kids as an enigmatic art/parent figure who calmly conveyed the importance of trusting

TOP LEFT: Eli Janney showing the quarter-inch tape of very early (1989) Girls Against Boys, 2021. Photo by Brendan Canty. TOP CENTER: Eli Janney, High Back Chairs *Of Two Minds* session, 1990–91. Photo by Charles Steck. TOP RIGHT: Eli having breakfast during High Back Chairs *Of Two Minds* session. Photo by Charles Steck. BOTTOM LEFT: Girls Against Boys, *Tropic of Scorpio* (1991) track sheet. Photo by Brendan Canty, 2021. BOTTOM RIGHT: Don (left) and Eli visiting Inner Ear, 2021. Photo by Brendan Canty.

in our own creative vision. The Arlington basement studio was small, and full of normal household objects—including Don's surfboard. There was nothing "music industry" there. It was semi-pro, self-taught, and beautifully home-built, which were all familiar values in the punk scene. But you couldn't help noticing that each fader, knob, patch bay, and tape box was properly labeled. Every recorded event was clearly documented on paper track sheets, and the tape machines were cleaned daily. There was no chaos on the studio side. Don's disembodied voice would warmly announce your song title ("take one") in your headphones, and the tape rolled. With teenage nerves temporarily under control, it was time for you to perform, or die.

A key ingredient in any creative collaboration is trust. Trust leads you to a place like Inner Ear. Perhaps your local heroes had already made explosive recordings down in Don's basement, now maybe it was your turn. When Don moved the microphones around your gear to capture your trashy guitar sound, or razor-cut and reassembled your fragile master tape from tiny pieces into a finished order, it was magic, and you believed in it. When my band Gray Matter first went into Inner Ear in '84, we had only the burning desire to make a recording and be heard. When we walked out, thanks to Don (and Ian), we had made a freaking album!

These experiences at Inner Ear were formative and inspired me to build my own community-based recording studio, and to pursue a lengthy career in audio engineering. Don's encouragement and affability while working with others set the blueprint that I still draw upon in my work and my life to this day.

Chad Clark

Sound Engineer and Producer / Beauty Pill

"IT'S GONNA *BE* THAT WAY"

In the early '90s when I was a kid, Don Zientara invited me to assist him on some sessions as an engineer. This was basically an internship, although we never called it that. It was a fantastic opportunity and it certainly changed my life.

What I learned from those early sessions was more of a spirit and mindset than a technical approach. As an engineer, Don is playful and improvisatory. He does have some techniques—certain pieces of gear he returns to sometimes, certain microphones he favors on certain instruments, etc.—but he mostly reinvents his process every day. He's not particularly preoccupied with formulas or recipes.

And you know what? Don's true mastery is not technical at all. Don's true mastery is the art of making people comfortable. That's where his idiosyncratic genius lies. The art of making people comfortable is a very deep and complex art, but Don makes it seem simple.

One of my favorite Don Zientara anecdotes comes from a session I observed when I was a kid: Don was recording a hard rock band, I can't remember their name. They were mediocre and forgettable. This story isn't really about them.

In the session, Don seemed as cheerful and present as he always does. He never condescended to them, nor did he overly flatter them. He just . . . went about his work, helping them make a recording of their songs.

At one point, the guitarist wanted to overdub a guitar solo. He began setting up a chain of guitar pedals. To me, the sound seemed to get worse with the addition of each successive pedal.

Finally, the guitarist turned to face the control room and said, "How's that?" This was an awkward moment. It sounded really bad. Like unbelievably bad.

In a plain and even tone, Don said, "The thing is . . . if you *play* it that way, it's going to be that way."

The guitarist paused and said, "Yeah." And he began calmly removing the pedals out of the signal chain.

To me, this was a wholly oblique exchange. Honestly, I *still* don't quite understand it all these years later. Sort of a Jedi mind trick or an abstract Zen koan. Felt almost arcane. Everything was communicated in tone and cadence.

The main takeaway was that the musician was not insulted or upset. And Don had gently coaxed him toward a better result without hurting his feelings.

Not easy to do! You try it sometime.

"EVERY TOY IN ITS PLACE"

Something most people notice: Inner Ear resembles a child's playhouse.

Something most people miss: Inner Ear is an extremely *orderly* place.

It's important to note that both things are true and the two traits are tightly interrelated.

There are toys, puzzles, and stuffed animals everywhere. It's lovely and perfect in this way. The statement, which everyone feels immediately, is, *Creativity is play. Play is welcome here. Go ahead and be a kid.*

But underlying that statement, there is a fastidious attention to detail. The toys aren't "strewn all around," they are *selected* and *placed*. It's not a dirty or messy "rock and roll studio." Everything runs like clockwork. Nothing about its design is desultory. It's all deliberate.

The equipment is exactingly maintained and I can tell you a little secret: Don installed little mirrors on the back of most of the gear, so he can see what he's doing when reaching behind it. (Ingenious, right? So simple! Why doesn't everyone do this? I don't know!)

One of the things I learned early on working at Inner Ear was the right way to coil microphone cords so they last longer. I'm quite bad at it. When I fucked it up, Don would call me out on it. As he should.

So I can tell you what feels like a playful and carefree environment actually has rigor, design, and intention behind it. And it's all in service of making people comfortable, which as I said before is Don's true art.

If the studio were chaotic or slovenly, it would be less inspiring and more constraining. I believe that very strongly.

"KEEP GOING!"

I worked at Inner Ear for a decade. I had my own smaller adjoining studio called Silver Sonya. This was during a period when my life was in flux. My band Beauty Pill had released an album called *The Unsustainable Lifestyle*. The music went far afield of the aesthetics of rock music and not everyone loved it. It was mostly met with bad reviews and listener indifference. This failure was painful and it affected me. I began to question myself and my future in music. The band disintegrated.

I went through an intense depression. But I had to go to work in the studio every day. Life doesn't stop when you get depressed, as much as you might like it to. You still gotta get up in the morning, you still gotta make a living

In a way, I tried to bury the part of myself that was an artist during this period. I just wanted to work at a studio and do the work I was paid to do. I wanted to let go of my identity as songwriter and musician. I wanted to just be a technician for hire.

However, at night, I found myself staying at the studio, experimenting with a new mode of music: electronic. I was messing around with new software and instruments . . . and I was headed even further away from rock music than *The Unsustainable Lifestyle*. For about a year, I made an abstract jumble of impressionistic sounds and noises.

Pursuing this direction certainly felt like "career suicide," insofar as I had a music career at all. But I wanted to do it. Something inside was compelling me forward. I can't explain it.

I toiled obsessively and alone, sometimes till almost dawn. A song began to emerge. This was exciting, but I felt extreme self-doubt. *What the hell am I doing? Who is this music for? What is the point? What am I doing with my life?*

How our studios were structured, Don had to walk past my door on his way out to the parking lot. Late one night, he stopped in the doorway and listened to what I was doing. I felt embarrassed for anyone to hear it.

Don stood there listening for a few seconds and then he said, "Amazing."

"What the hell am I doing, Don? I really don't know!" I said, feeling lost and bewildered and tired.

"You're making Chad Clark music!" he said sweetly. In a way, this was a simple statement of fact. But there was something distinctly warm and consoling in his tone. And it was a warmth I really needed to feel at that moment. Don's not an overly sentimental guy, but I could feel his genuine positivity.

"Thanks, Don."

Don added, "Keep going!" And he spun out to the parking lot.

The world is unkind to artists. Nobody encourages you to take chances. Nobody encourages you to explore the unknown.

You're mostly on your own. But, simple as it was, this moment with Don meant the world. It was late at night. I'm sure I looked deranged and exhausted, but Don didn't say, "Go home, Chad." He said, "Keep going."

The song I was working on ultimately became Beauty Pill's "Ann the Word," an artistic breakthrough that would change my life and open up new realms of opportunity. It's certainly now one of the best-known and most beloved Beauty Pill songs. It influenced the direction of *Beauty Pill Describes Things as They Are*, which is by far the most successful album of my life. And it led to a film- and theater-scoring career.

There's nothing conspicuously "punk" about "Ann," aesthetically. Nobody thinks of it as a "typical Inner Ear song," but I'm here to tell you it couldn't have happened anywhere else.

I'm grateful to Inner Ear Studio.

J. Robbins

Sound Engineer and Producer / Jawbox - Channels

Jawbox recorded at Inner Ear many times. We did our first album there, *Grippe*, with Eli Janney engineering, and we did our second full-length there, *Novelty*, with Don assisting Iain Burgess (Chicago-based engineer/producer who worked with Naked Raygun and many other of our favorite bands at the time), and we did one more single there, "Motorist," with Don and Ian.

A more recent band of mine, Channels, recorded one song with Don, and it was such fun to work with him. And for me it was a treat to not be the engineer on the session, but simply to play music and to know we were in good hands.

After Jawbox broke up in 1996, Don gave me the chance to run the B studio there, which was a second control room housing all the gear that used to be in his basement. I learned so much in that space, recorded so many good bands and projects. It was the cheaper option for recording at Inner Ear, thanks to the weird half-inch sixteen-track analog format and the very small control room. Gradually I moved into doing work in the main studio on two-inch twenty-four-track. Don was a great mentor, and had such patience with my sometimes haphazard ways.

The microphone closet alone was a great education for a budding engineer, since Don had such a vast selection of mics, some that were sort of "legendary" and rare. it was an opportunity to find out what worked best, and what I liked, from a wide range of possibilities. In Studio B there was the old Tascam console from the basement version of Inner Ear, but there was also a much simpler homemade passive mixer that Don built himself, which sounded superb. It was a real lesson in how simpler is often better, and the appearance of slickness is so often a distraction. It wasn't long before I was relying heavily on that homemade mixer and bypassing the Tascam as much as I could. Don was also great at finding good and musical uses for equipment that wasn't always considered "top of the range"—he taught me that your ears really are the most important piece of equipment you have as an engineer.

But Don's greatest legacy in recording, and as a teacher, is in his attitude. He really connects with people, he trusts musicians, and he trusts the moment. He cares about the sound, but he understands that capturing the *energy* of a performance or a personality is paramount. When we're listening to music, it's not the frequencies or the compression or the mics or any bit of gear we're listening to—what's compelling us is a kind of communication that doesn't happen any other way than through music. The studio needs to be a nurturing environment rather than an intimidating one, to help foster confidence and connection—the studio is there for the artist and the art, not the other way around. When I first met Don I was obsessed by certain sounds, and so focused on capturing them in a certain way, and it took me a long time to really absorb that wisdom, which was right there in front of me, that it's about *people*. I think everyone who ever worked with Don has learned these kinds of life lessons from him, by observation or experience. For me, Inner Ear was not just a place where I learned a lot and did formative work, it was like a microcosmic university of life.

Don (left) and TJ Lipple, recording session for David Zaidain, 2021. Photo by Antonia Tricarico.

TJ Lipple

Sound Engineer and Producer / Aloha

Every independently owned recording studio is a reflection of the mind of its owner. When you're in their studio, you are in their head. The decor, signal path, and gear selection are an extension of the person who set it up and laid it out. Inner Ear is a comfortable place, like a friend's basement hangout, where you can make a record without realizing it. On the walls is a mishmash of found art, hand-painted sets from one of Don's grandkids' school plays, alongside his own art—paint and pencil, somewhat abstract malformed human figures . . . way darker art than you would expect if you knew the guy. He keeps his surfboard on top of an acoustic cloud in the live room. The studio gear spans a crazy range of quality from priceless to worthless, but to Don it's practically all the same. The Crate amp he found on the corner waiting for trash pickup is just as valuable as his 1950s tweed Fender Champ and certainly gets more use from him. And that's just remarkable, to have such an open mind and also good taste. Maybe the same non-snobby attitude that drew me in was also what attracted the Teen Idles way back when.

One day I walked in the studio, and Don was trying to repair that old Champ amp in the tool room just opposite his control room. (He has built his own reverb unit and compressor, and has wired his entire studio . . . he knows circuits and solder.) It's a small amp with pretty simple circuitry, as far as that goes. He went through every component with no luck. Finally he smacked the thing, and voilà! Back in business. He was tickled.

I first met Don briefly in 1996, I think, when my high school band visited from central Pennsylvania while looking for a studio to record. (Our demo tape is still in his office.) We arranged to meet with Don and another local DC engineer. I remember posing the naive question, "Do you like every band you record?" The other engineer said something to the effect of, "HAHA, no." But Don said yes, he did. If you can imagine the wide scope of music—and attempts at music—an experienced recording engineer will encounter, you understand that this is kind of a profound statement. And if you know Don, you know he means it.

I moved to Arlington from Pittsburgh in 2002 and joined Chad Clark in renting the front room at Inner Ear, where Eli Janney and J. Robbins had been before. Chad and I rented that space from Don until 2007. I continued to run many sessions, first at Inner Ear and then also at Bastille, which took our place in the front room. My band Aloha recorded three records and one EP at Inner Ear. I also played drums for the Del Ray Desperadoes, which is Don's cover band that he's played in since the 1970s with his old friends from the National Gallery of Art in DC.

My last session at Inner Ear is tomorrow (August 7, 2021). I'm not a very sentimental person, but I do feel sad imagining it gone. It was my second home for almost twenty years. But the building is just that: a building. Inner Ear is Don.

Cati Sesana
Sound Engineer

I met Don in October 2017 when I enrolled in the Recording Connection School for Audio Engineering.

We had an interview to make sure we were a good match and we hit it off. I did the program for two years, during which he taught me one-on-one how to record in the studio and mixing postproduction. I had done an internship in another studio but never got to learn how to actually do everything until Don taught me. I came in with minimal knowledge but eventually I was able to bring in people to record on my own, and when I completed the program I stayed on as a freelance engineer.

Don is such a kind and patient teacher, and the education I got through him has opened doors to new opportunities that would not have been possible before. Learning directly from Don at Inner Ear is a once-in-a-lifetime experience and I am honored to be his apprentice. It is absolutely heartbreaking that Inner Ear has closed because there is so much DC music history in this studio. It is such an ironic shame that this historic site will cease to exist to make way for a new arts center. I will miss the studio, but most of all I will miss hanging out with my mentor and friend.

Cati Sesana

TOP LEFT: Cati Sesana at the mixing desk. TOP RIGHT: Aiko posing at the mixing desk, 2021. BOTTOM: Cati Sesana (left) and Don, 2021. Photos by Cati Sesana.

Wilfredo Morales

Double Sharp Audio / Maple

I met Don in the early aughts at the tender age of sixteen. The producer and warlock Darin "Flame" Drake liked my band, Maple, and funded a session at Inner Ear.

Don was welcoming and kind to this maladjusted, angsty teen. He's always quick with a joke, quip ready at the hip. Don, being a foodie, kept us fed throughout the session. Being in that calming environment left an impression on me. I wanted a career in music and Inner Ear demonstrated it didn't have to be competitive or exclusive. We kept in touch over the years as Don and I shared gigs in the area.

I moved into the front office of Inner Ear in May 2021 to conduct music lessons and record bands. News of the studio closure began to circulate around this time, but Don has encouraged me with his positive mental attitude and consistent productivity.

Don and Alex Vidales invited me to join *StageCraft*, a program hosted at Inner Ear and broadcast on WERA 96.7 FM with Amanda Dove, Fred Hof, Giovanni Tario, and MJ Willis. The team welcomed me as a performer and accompanist with open arms. Between anecdotes and banter, Don provides listeners with a masterclass on sound, performance, and the philosophy of simple living.

Don always makes time for others and speaks to everybody as an equal, without pretense. My fellow engineers Deb Edattel, Sangmo Werner, Josh Roberts, and I regularly bug him with technical questions and debate the merits of different snacks (Don views chips as the superior snack). I'll endeavor to emulate his mentorship and patience with my own music students, clients, and friends.

As a kid, sitting at my desk in school—bored and restless—I used to daydream about working at Inner Ear. In my brief but spectacular time there, I've pulled all-night recording

Skeeter Thompson solo session, 2021. (Left to right) Skeeter Thompson, Wilfredo Morales, and Don. Photo by John Kelly.

sessions, smoked with the rhythm section of Scream, politely argued with Ian MacKaye over Jimi Hendrix's Hawaii concerts, and practiced and worked harder than I ever have. Artists come here to work, play, and collaborate in a space where they're free to be themselves. Inner Ear was that rare bastion of creativity in the community.

At the time of this writing, Don and I are looking forward to performing a farewell concert the day after the doors close. We plan to keep the fun going.

TOP: *StageCraft* live in the Inner Ear alley, 2021. (Left to right) Joey Jenkins, Alex Alavi, Don, MJ Willis, Wilfredo Morales, Alex Vidales, Fred Hoff, and Giovanni Tario (front). Photo by John Stevens. BOTTOM: *StageCraft* crew outside Inner Ear, 2021. (Left to right) Aiko the dog, Cati Sesana, Fred Hoff, Don, MJ Willis, Wilfredo Morales, and Alex Vidales (seated). Photo by James Willis.

Alex Vidales

StageCraft

Don and I decided to start a public radio show because we thought it would be a good way to help artists develop in ways that would build a larger and more engaged audience. It ended up becoming a performance all by itself—we became pseudo-radio personalities. Over the past five years of our weekly radio program, *StageCraft,* we have interviewed over two hundred artists of all kinds, exploring every detail of what goes on before, during, and even after a performance.

During the summers, we would do live versions of *StageCraft* in the alley behind Inner Ear, and things always got a bit out of hand. In the top picture to the left, you see me wearing a silk robe that was busted out because someone had taken offense at a tank top I'd worn the week before. We also introduced in this episode the "Open Mic of Doom" where we would spin a wheel and we had to perform whatever the wheel landed on, be it a song, a poem, juggling, or even a rap about history.

Meeting Don the first time and getting his advice was a gift; being able to work for a year in Inner Ear was a joy; his agreement to do a public radio show with me was an honor—but the time we had a beer together to celebrate our second year doing the show, when he told me that he loved doing the show because it was fun, was one of the best days of my life.

Afterword

Juanita Zientara

Don today is the guy he's always been: an artist, a musician, an all-around good man. We met in 1974. I was in the process of adopting a toddler from Vietnam. (Don's birthday, I later learned, was #1 in the draft lottery.) Don was looking for someone to ride bikes with. And so we did. Then came camping, frying hamburgers on a hibachi on the back porch of my group house, and long evenings listening to him playing his Gibson from the squishy comfort of our beanbag chairs. He never questioned the adoption, other than to cheer me on. About a year later we welcomed Emily together when she landed at National Airport. He quietly seemed to be sticking around. "Dong . . . vmmm, vmmm, *vmmm!*" Em would soon babble! Toddler translation: "Don's arriving on his motorcycle!"

Em spoke no English but she was a chatterbox in Vietnamese. And she was constantly in motion. One afternoon, while twirling around as she often did, she careened smack into Don's Gibson. *Bam!* The neck cracked and Don's only comment was a cool, "I'll have to get it fixed." No anger, no frustration. Just calm. *Good dad material!* I thought. Well, we married and such a fine dad he's been.

Throughout his tenure at the National Gallery, Don was respectfully known as Doctor Z. He brought competence, kindness, patience, and focus to every project, assisting his colleagues in the details of mounting major exhibits. During the day he assisted the gallery exhibit staff and eventually he ran their sound studio. Don's love of art and sound production had merged. At night he began constructing a modest studio of his own here at home. "Build it and they will come." And come musicians did! So add "audio engineer" and "carpenter" to his résumé.

To our daughters, Emily and Kate, their dad is Mr. Fix It . . . the person they can reliably count on. He encouraged the kids to solve problems as far as they could before stepping in. I think he directs his recording sessions that way, sorting out with the musicians what they want to create and then figuring out how they can best realize their vision.

Don's love of art, music, and the mysterious potential of electronics is clearly apparent. As a kid, he haunted thrift shops hunting for discarded amps and speakers to dismantle and resurrect to better form. On South Ivy Street our nondescript basement held promise. Our little home became an incubator for so many bands, punk and beyond.

"Living above the store" had its challenges. I was an ESL teacher, facing long hours of prep and often coursework each evening. More importantly, we were raising two young daughters. I'm not a musician. I feel my contribution to Inner Ear's growth was to just go about each day as needed. Mom, teacher, confidante. Don and I communicated freely and if heavy drumming ran too often late into the night, we'd have *the talk*. The very positive aspects of having the studio running at home full-time were many. Don could be on call. Our girls met countless fine musicians (some fairly young themselves) who were amazingly tolerant of the shenanigans of kids.

I remember these years as a family being incredibly full and rich. Memories: Don escorting both girls to preschool each morning on his Suzuki. Minor Threat once playing during the kids' school fair in the '80s. Don and Kate often riding bikes on the George Washington bike trail. Cheering Don on as he competed in triathlons on the Eastern Shore. Our family life was sacred and we hope our chosen work built a good foundation for our daughters' lives. By the time Don had left the National Gallery and moved Inner Ear to South Oakland, the girls were older and the open lower level, free of commitments, was naturally a welcomed space to expand.

Don is a gifted, hardworking artist. He has spent his life mastering the art of recording and he's used his gift for the good. He is also a beautiful musician. His songs are poetry; he sings from his heart. I still love nothing better than listening to him playing that same Gibson. Bringing Inner Ear back home seems right.

TOP LEFT: Juanita Zientara, 2019. RIGHT: Emily Zientara-Harvey, 1987. BOTTOM: Kate in the basement studio, 1989. Photos courtesy of Juanita Zientara.

Kate Zientara-Whitney

It can be hard to go back in time, but what I remember about the basement studio, as Don's youngest daughter, is going downstairs and hanging on the pipes and listening to all the takes and playbacks. Looking through the plexiglass at bands playing and in between the plexiglass was Mr. Frog (rubber, of course, lol) hanging out. Then, when bands would take breaks, going outside with them like they were my big brothers and really acting like I knew what was going on. It was life and we went with the flow just doing what we did. It is amazing that it is now back where it all started from.

Emily Zientara-Harvey

How about I tell you the story of an unassuming home, in a suburb of DC, with rust-colored shag carpeting, hosting one of the most significant studios in DC's punk movement . . . That was my house.

Growing up, I had no idea the impact my father was making in this field. My dad: the motorcycle-riding, flip-flop-wearing tallest guy I'd ever seen, and thus the best Igor at Halloween, with the sense of humor of a fourteen-year-old boy, who was in fact moonlighting as a rather high-profile sound technician to pretty much this whole underground scene. Meanwhile upstairs, we crept around the main floor on the aforementioned carpeting so as not to "add" to the full-bodied and raucous music being created downstairs. For a long time, the side porch off the living room doubled as a control room, casually put together by drilling a hole directly through the floor for mic wires going to the basement; the window from the living room was the best seat in the house to view the show.

While I knew what my father was doing was cool . . . I was far from that. In fact, my designation in middle school was "the girl with the recording studio in her basement." The acknowledgment allowed me a semblance of credibility that, had I any grasp of it at the time, would have been a teen girl's dream. Later, when punk was really becoming THE movement in DC, I'd mostly graduated on to the "popular" music of the time. Coming home to see young men sitting around in my living room, in remnants of my dress-up box, blasé. Having a musician of whatever band cook me dinner, passé. Seeing history-making music during creation, so what. If you see it every day, it loses its significance. I wanted to wash clothes in the basement, and to stomp through the living room just because my dad's "hobby" took such precedence. I displayed utter cluelessness and lack of tact in being a teenager and I realize now the beauty and kindness of the many musicians who did not mind my lack of manners. I really don't think much about those years because in the context of all of this, I was still just a teenager. My dad was just my dad, and the studio was his extra job in the basement. Some nights I'd go to bed to music and wake up to music, and that was okay.

Some stories I like to tell are about the numerous times I came home from school to see punks, straight-edge punks, sitting in my living room waiting for their turn in the studio below. How about the time my dad picked Mom, Kate, and me up at the airport sans glasses? He'd lost them in the Ontario Theater mosh pit. Then there were the times we were not allowed to sneak downstairs because the singer liked to record in the nude, and yeah, Joey Picuri making me and Kate pasta in my mom's old kitchen.

TOP ROW: studio gear disassembly, 2021. Photos by Antonia Tricarico. BOTTOM LEFT: mixing room dismantling, 2021. BOTTOM CENTER: hallway dismantling, 2021. BOTTOM RIGHT: living room wall dismantling, 2021. Photos by Juanita Zientara.

Taking down the doorbell and mailbox, 2021.
Photo by Juanita Zientara.

Inner Ear, 2022. TOP LEFT: new basement control room. TOP RIGHT: new Allen & Heath forty-eight-track mixer. BOTTOM LEFT: project screen detail. BOTTOM RIGHT: new digital work bench. Photos by John Stevens.

TOP: Don surfing at Frisco Village, Cape Hatteras, NC, 2009. BOTTOM: Don with old perforated steel plate, Cape Hatteras, 2019. Photos by John Stevens.

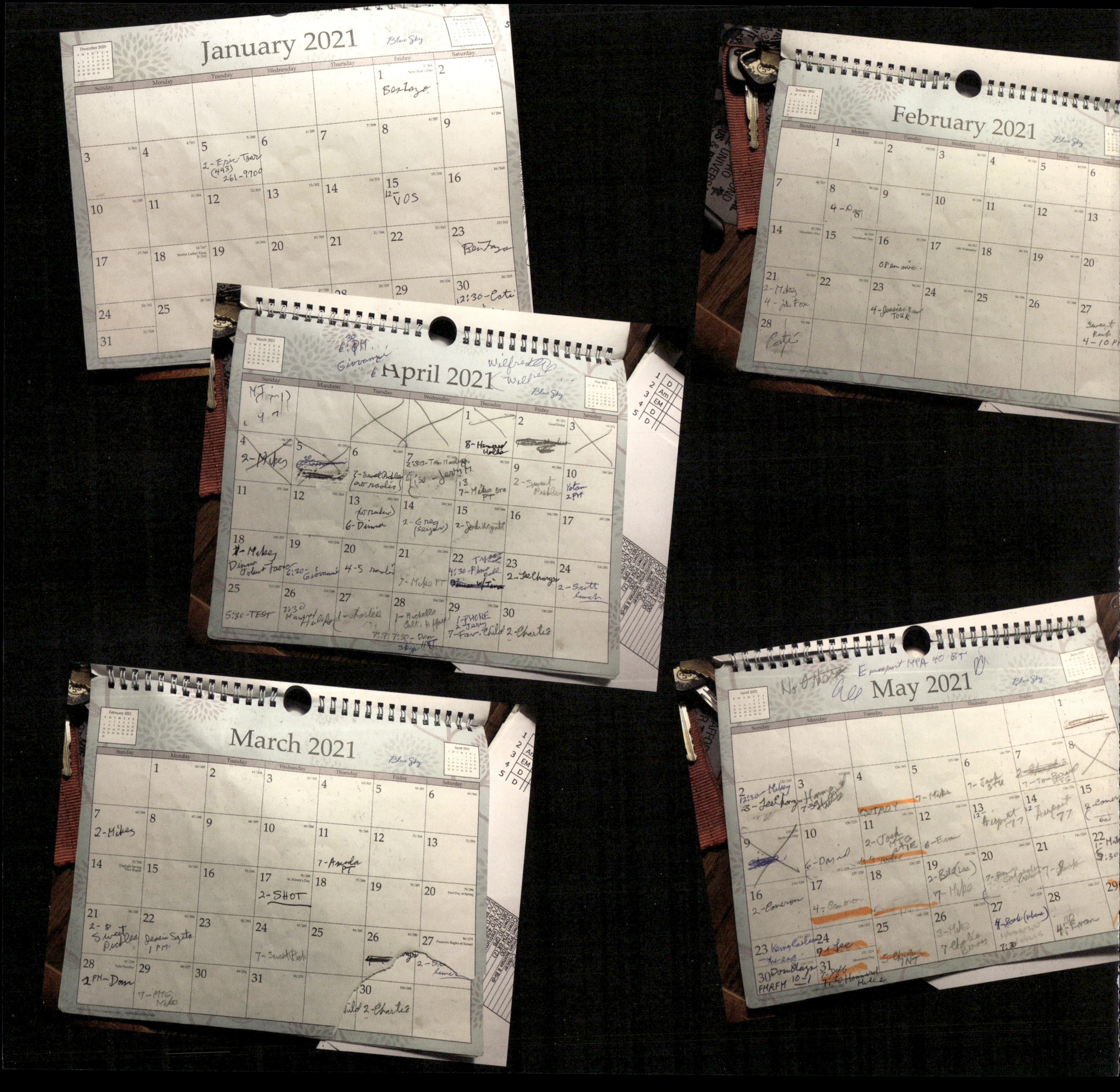

January 2021

February 2021

April 2021

March 2021

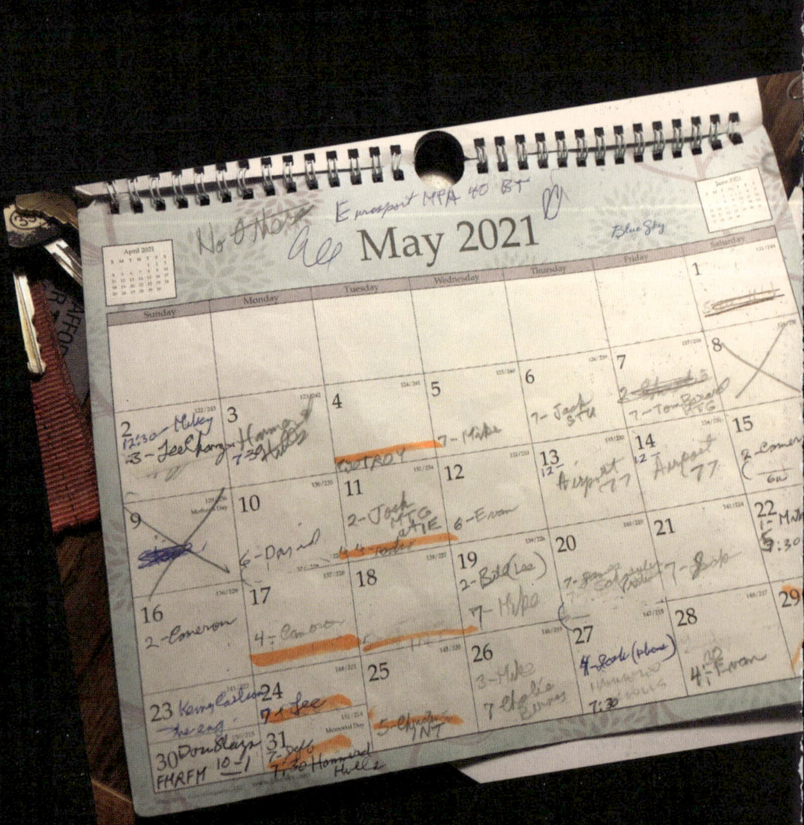